Cook's Voyages
and
Peoples of the Pacific

Cook's Voyages
and
Peoples of the Pacific

EDITED BY
Hugh Cobbe

Published for the Trustees of the British Museum
and the British Library Board by
British Museum Publications Limited

© 1979, The Trustees of the British Museum and the British Library Board
ISBN 0 7141 1550 9 *cased*
ISBN 0 7141 1551 7 *paper*
Published by British Museum Publications Ltd
6 Bedford Square, London WC1B 3RA

British Library Cataloguing in Publication Data

Cook's voyages and peoples of the Pacific.
1. Cook, James, b. 1728   2. Pacific Ocean – Exploring expeditions   3. Ethnology – Pacific area
4. Pacific area – Social life and customs
I. Cobbe, Hugh   II. British Museum   III. British Library
910'.09'164   G.420.C65

The map of Cook's Three Voyages is reproduced from Rex and Thea Rienits, *The Voyages of Captain Cook*, by courtesy of The Hamlyn Publishing Group Ltd.

Designed by Brian Paine
Set in 12 on 14 Monophoto Garamond 156 by Filmtype Services Limited, Scarborough and London
Printed in Great Britain by W S Cowell Ltd

Contents

List of Colour Plates   6

Acknowledgements   7

Map of Cook's Three Voyages   8

The Authors   10

Introduction   11

1 The Voyages and their Background   13

2 The Society Islands   47

3 New Zealand   71

4 The Nootka of Vancouver Island   89

5 Hawaii   109

6 Conclusion   129

References and Abbreviations   143

List of Colour Plates

[*Between pages* 72 *and* 73]

I Captain James Cook by John Webber, artist on the Third Voyage.

II *Resolution* and *Discovery* in Christmas Harbour, Kerguelen Island, by John Webber, 1776.

III View on the island of 'Eimeo' (Moorea), Society Islands, by John Webber, 1777.

IV Breast gorget, comprising a basketry base with feathers, shark-teeth and dog hair. Society Islands.

V Two girls dancing in Tahiti, by John Webber, 1777.

VI Dress of the chief mourner. Society Islands.

VII Wood treasure box. New Zealand.

VIII Wood canoe bailer. New Zealand.

IX Bird-mask of wood. Nootka Sound.

X Wood bowl carved with two handles in the form of people. Nootka Sound.

XI Feather image of a god. Hawaiian Islands.

XII Feather image of a god. Hawaiian Islands.

XIII Feather helmet. Hawaiian Islands.

XIV Feather temple. Hawaiian Islands.

Acknowledgements

A number of persons and institutions lent objects or provided photographs both for use in the exhibition and in this book, and their kindness in doing so is acknowledged with gratitude. They are:

H.M. the Queen
Cambridge, University Museum of Archaeology and Ethnology
Cambridge, Massachusetts, Peabody Museum of Archaeology and Ethnology
Professor C. M. D. Crowder, Kingston, Ontario
Greenwich, National Maritime Museum
Hull, Warden and Brethren of the Hull Trinity House
London, British Museum (Natural History)
London, Public Record Office
London, Ministry of Defence (Navy)
Sydney, Mitchell Library, National Library of New South Wales
Mr and Mrs P. A. Tritton, Parham Park, West Sussex
Vienna, Museum für Völkerkunde
Dr J. C. Wright, Bernice P. Bishop Museum, Honolulu, Hawaii

The editor and authors of the present volume also wish to express their indebtedness to the following who provided information and assistance:

The Commonwealth Institute, London
B. A. L. Cranstone, Curator, Pitt Rivers Museum, Oxford
Dr Howard Ferguson, Cambridge
Dr A. L. Kaeppler, Bernice P. Bishop Museum, Honolulu
Dr Averil Lysaght, London
M. D. McLeod, Keeper, Museum of Mankind, London

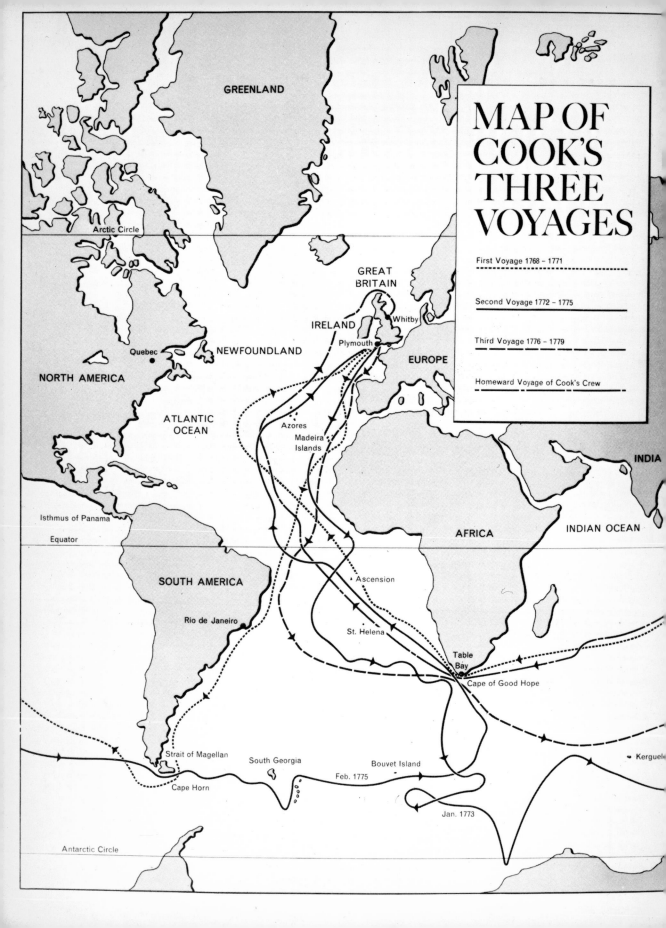

MAP OF COOK'S THREE VOYAGES

First Voyage 1768 – 1771

Second Voyage 1772 – 1775

Third Voyage 1776 – 1779

Homeward Voyage of Cook's Crew

GREENLAND

Arctic Circle

GREAT
BRITAIN

IRELAND

Whitby

Plymouth

EUROPE

Quebec

NEWFOUNDLAND

NORTH AMERICA

ATLANTIC
OCEAN

Azores

Madeira
Islands

INDIA

Isthmus of Panama

Equator

AFRICA

INDIAN OCEAN

SOUTH AMERICA

Ascension

Rio de Janeiro

St. Helena

Table
Bay

Cape of Good Hope

Strait of Magellan

South Georgia

Bouvet Island

Feb. 1775

Kerguele

Cape Horn

Jan. 1773

Antarctic Circle

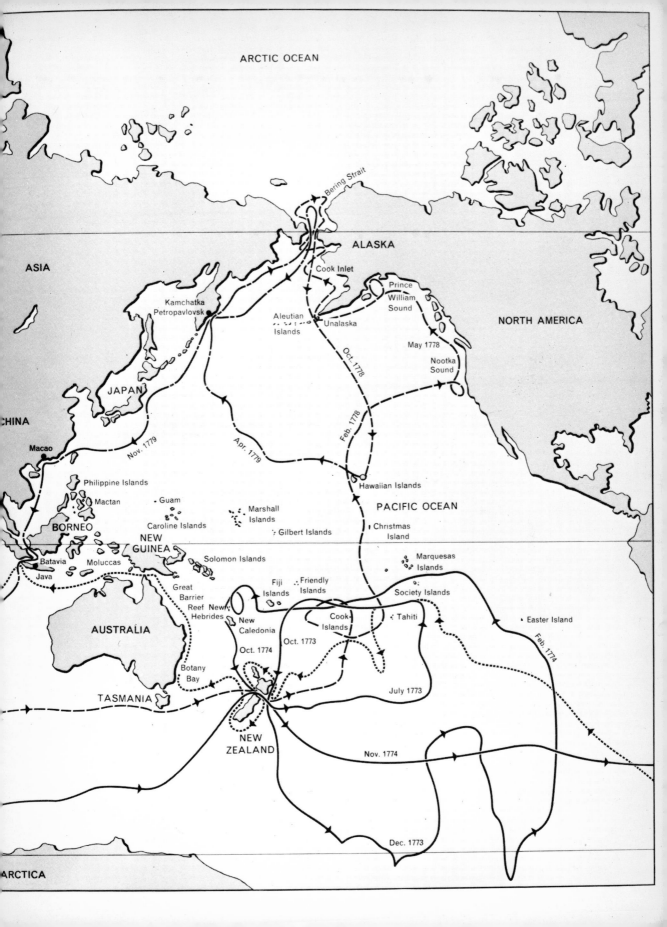

The Authors

Hugh Cobbe (editor, author of Chapter 1) was, at the time of writing, Assistant Keeper in the Department of Manuscripts, British Library, responsible for the collection of maps and geographical manuscripts there; J. C. H. King (Chapter 4) is Assistant Keeper in the Museum for Mankind responsible for the North American collection; Dorota Czarkowska Starzecka (Chapters 2, 3, 5) is Assistant Keeper in the Museum of Mankind responsible for the Oceanic collection; Dr Helen Wallis (Chapter 6) is Map Librarian in the British Library.

Introduction

THERE can be little doubt that the climax of geographical achievement in the eighteenth century was the opening up of the Pacific Ocean. An area which had hitherto been an almost unexplored tract, full of infinite possibility and potential in terms of geography, trade and territorial expansion, became known for what it was, a huge expanse of water with many islands but only two major land masses, Australia and New Zealand. The explorer who was responsible more than any other for revealing this was Captain James Cook. In three great voyages he provided solutions to questions about the Southern Hemisphere which had been asked (and often answered, but wrongly) for centuries, ever since man had first started speculating about the nature of the unknown parts of the earth.

These solutions may have been disappointing, in terms of the comparatively small amount of land discovered, as will be seen in Chapter 1, but in the course of his explorations he came across societies and cultures of which Europe had hitherto known little or nothing: the flourishing Polynesian civilisation of Oceania; the Indians of the Pacific coast of North America; the Melanesian cultures of the western Pacific, and the aboriginal population of Australia.

The bicentenary of Cook's death in Hawaii on 14 February 1779 prompted the organisation of an exhibition in which an attempt was made to illustrate the nature and the consequences of this encounter, which was such a revelation at the time. One must imagine a minute group of Europeans in one or two small ships isolated in the vastness of the Pacific Ocean, knowing little of its geography and almost nothing of its inhabitants, half the world away from home, suffering all the privations of a long voyage: shortage of food, no variety in diet, the psychological strain of spending months at a time in cramped quarters out of sight of land in climates ranging from the intense heat and humidity of the tropics to the harsh frozen emptiness of the Antarctic. In sharp contrast to the rigours of the voyages was the seemingly peaceful idyllic existence of the islanders. So great was its impact that these people were described in great detail, first by the trained scientist, Joseph Banks, and then by

Cook and his other companions in their journals which have ever since attracted wide interest.

Cook was a keen and perceptive observer with a scrupulous regard for truth, and as the voyages progress we find his interest in the native peoples increasing to a point where, on a visit to Tonga, he participated in a ceremony stripped to the waist with his hair loose. Although he was not to know it (though he and Banks were certainly apprehensive on this score) he was depicting a world which the consequences of his visit were to debase and all but destroy. The exhibition was designed to present his picture of this world and as an adjunct to the exhibition the present book is planned as a commentary drawing on the same material, but in a different way.

In the British Museum was collected the finest surviving collection of material derived from Cook's voyages (it is now divided between three institutions, see p.46) and both the exhibition and the book are based on this collection. There are highly important items of Cook material in many other places, but the British Museum collection, taken as a whole, is so rich that it was necessary to borrow very little from elsewhere.

The plan of the book is simple: an initial chapter sketches in the background to the voyages, attempting to provide a brief explanation of how they came about with an outline of Cook's previous career, and an account of the voyages in a chronological framework. The following chapters discuss the four most important cultures encountered by Cook: those of the Society Islanders, the Maori of New Zealand, the Nootka Indians of Vancouver Island and the Hawaiians. The cultures are described in the light of modern ethnology and the events of Cook's visit, or visits, are related. A final chapter sums up the impact of the South Sea world on Europe and of European influence on the South Sea.

H. C.

1 *The Voyages and their Background*

HUGH COBBE

I
F one imagines oneself to be, say, a sixteenth-century thinker with little concrete
information on the southern hemisphere, but with a reasonably clear idea of the
geography of the northern, one would naturally be inclined to suppose that it
was much the same. It would comprise mostly land, though there might be a belt of
water girdling the earth at the equator. True, there might also be some large oceans,
as indeed there was the Atlantic Ocean in the northern hemisphere between Europe
and the recently discovered American continent, but one would expect the greater
part to be land; in this way was created in the popular imagination the *Terra Australis
Incognita* which had of necessity to exist to balance the land masses of the north.

The history of the world-map is a slow progress from the early examples, such as
those based on Ptolemy or Macrobius (where the world is depicted schematically in a
manner that bears little relation to reality and owes less to information than to
speculation), through a series of ever increasing likenesses down to the accurate
maps of the present day. It is surprising for how long cartographers were willing to
blemish (in our eyes) otherwise reasonably accurate representations of the southern
hemisphere with large continents marked *Terra Australis Incognita,* or even (so
powerful was the force of the intellectual assumption) *Terra Australis nondum Cognita*
('Southern land not yet known'). Information provided by the voyages of Magellan
(1520–22), or by those commissioned by Spain in the later part of the sixteenth and
early part of the seventeenth centuries (Mendaña, Quiros and Torres) and those of
the Dutch in the middle of the seventeenth century (Schouten and Lemaire, Tasman)
gradually reduced the possible area of the posited continent. More and more open
sea was discovered and those pieces of land which were charted on first discovery as
part of the Great Southern Continent (e.g. Tierra del Fuego, Java and New Holland
[Australia]), were found on further enquiry to be islands and not at all northern
projections of a huge land-mass in the south. The so-called Harley World-Map [1]
dating from the 1540s shows Tierra del Fuego and Java treated in this way ('Le
Terre Australle' and 'Jave la Grande' respectively).

[13]

1 (*overleaf*) Section of the Harley World Map, showing
part of the conjectured Great Southern Continent
projecting north to south-east Asia. Dieppe
School, *c.*1540–50. *Add. MS 5413*

IAVE LA GRANDE:

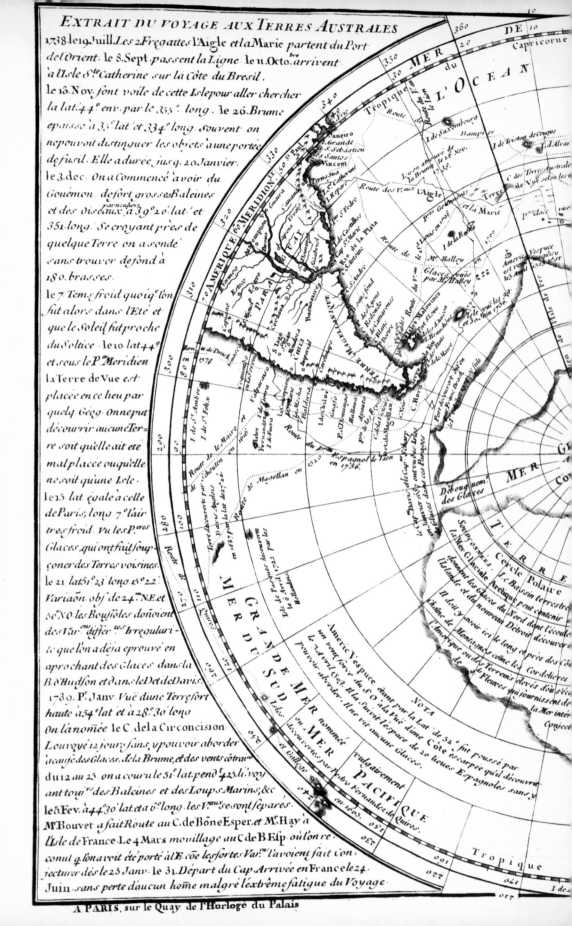

2 Philippe Bauche: *Carte des Terres Australes*. The 1754 edition showing New Zealand as part of an antarctic continent. *K. Top. iv 60*

By the early years of the eighteenth century the idea of the continent still flourished [2], despite the fact that exploration by the Spanish and the Dutch, far from establishing its existence in the real world, had done little but diminish its potential size by increasing the known area where it could not be. It was the century in which England was seeking areas for economic expansion, and the riches that such a continent would bestow on its possessor were enticing indeed. Exploitation of the known parts of the Pacific was firmly in the hands of the Spanish or Dutch so British eyes turned to the unknown (which nonetheless surely existed).

If the Great Southern Continent was one geographical chimaera of the times, the North-West Passage was another. The theory that between Hudson's Bay in Canada and somewhere on the north-west coast of America there existed a sea passage was a notion clung to with as much tenacity as that of the continent, a tenacity born of the repugnance of the difficulties to be encountered when sailing through the straits of Magellan or around the Horn. The discovery, possession and control of such a northern passage would be an economic boon which, taken together with the continental possibilities of the southern Pacific, dazzled with opportunity. The origins and history of these two great geographical will o'the wisps may be traced elsewhere; for our present purpose suffice it to say that they were bright enough to influence the British government to despatch a series of voyages of discovery to the Pacific in the later part of the eighteenth century. The results of these circumnavigations were not all that the most enthusiastic champions of the continent could have wished, but the sum total of their discoveries was of a significance on a level with that of the discovery of America by the Spanish some three centuries earlier.

The first of these voyages was under the command of the Hon. John Byron whose instructions were to seek a continent in the south Atlantic and to establish British possession of the Falkland Islands (discovered by Richard Hawkins in 1594 and of course considered initially as part of the continent). Thereafter he was to follow the west coast of South America northwards in search of the North-West Passage. Byron succeeded in making a record circumnavigation (June 1764–May 1766) and did indeed take possession of the Falkland Islands but achieved little else. On his return, his ship, the *Dolphin*, was despatched at once on a second voyage, this time under Captain Samuel Wallis, who had instructions to pass through the Straits of Magellan and to sail thence westward in search of the continent in the southern Pacific. He passed through the Straits with difficulty (it took from December 1766 to April 1767) and at once encountered a phenomenon that made the execution of his instructions virtually impossible. Constant westerly winds at the western approach to the Straits of Magellan make it impossible to sail due west to where the continent was supposed to be. Like all his predecessors he therefore turned north-west and on 23 June 1767 he discovered and landed at what he named King George's Island, a

3 View of Matavai Bay ('Port Royal Bay'), Tahiti, drawn on Wallis's voyage by George Pinnock, 1767. *Add. MS 15499 f.25*

name soon discarded in favour of the native Otaheite or Tahiti. He established a base at Port Royal Bay, later known as Matavai Bay [3], and during his stay there he established friendly relations with the native population. Byron had been instructed to 'cultivate a Friendship with the Inhabitants, if you shall find any, presenting them with such Trifles as they may value, and shewing them all possible civility and respect'. Wallis did not stay long at Tahiti, but both he and, after him, Cook took these instructions to heart.

Wallis returned to England via the East Indies and the Cape of Good Hope, arriving home in May 1768. He had fixed the position of Tahiti reasonably accurately [4] but in terms of the main purpose of his voyage he had achieved little. The impossibility of sailing west from the Horn meant that there was still ample room in

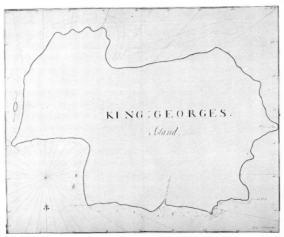

4 Chart of Tahiti by George Pinnock, 1767. Compare this with Cook's chart of 1769 (11). Both are drawn with the south at the top of the page. *Add. MS 15499 f.23*

[19]

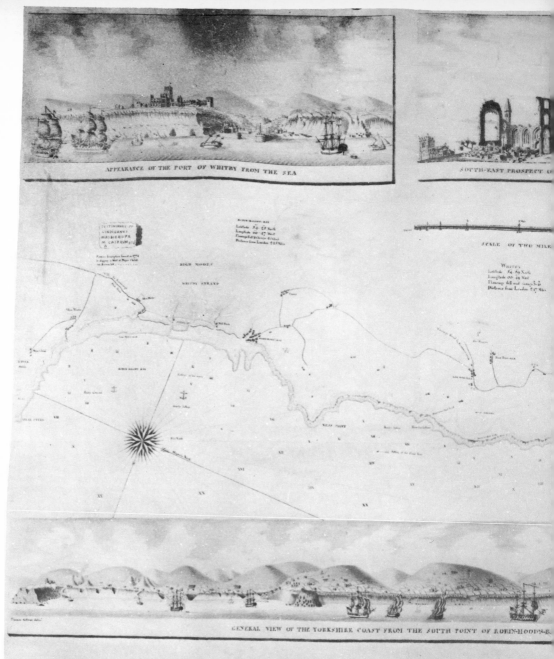

APPEARANCE OF THE PORT OF WHITBY FROM THE SEA

SOUTH-EAST PROSPECT OF

GENERAL VIEW OF THE YORKSHIRE COAST FROM THE SOUTH POINT OF ROBIN-HOOD'S-B

VIEW OF WHITBY FROM THE SOUTH.

OF WHITBY ABBEY

ENTRANCE OF RUNSWICK ROAD.

5 A composite
chart and view
of the Yorkshire
coast from
Robin Hood's Bay
to Runswick,
including Whitby,
by Francis Gibson,
1791.
K. Top. xliv 22

those waters for the continent, so that ideas expressed in Alexander Dalrymple's *An account of the discoveries made in the South Pacifick previous to 1764* (London, 1767, 88–103) which appeared in the year of Wallis' return and which had a section entitled 'Investigation of what may be farther expected in the South Sea' were by no means invalidated by the voyage. Dalrymple enumerates the high proportion of square degrees of land to water in the northern hemisphere which 'will probably be made up in the Southern Lands and Islands not yet discovered', and 'having shewn that there is a seeming necessity for a Southern Continent' he deduces, by citing various convenient sightings of land by the early voyagers, that the east side of the continent has already been discovered, that the west side is the west coast of New Zealand, which had been charted by Tasman in 1642, and asserts that all that remains is to discover the north coast. A further voyage was planned for this and another purpose (to which we shall come later), and to command it was chosen Mr James Cook, master of the schooner *Grenville* currently engaged on survey work in Newfoundland.

   The details of Cook's early life are to be found in any of a number of biographies: born on 27 October 1728 in the village of Marton-in-Cleveland, Yorkshire, the son of a Scottish labourer, he was apprenticed at seventeen to a grocer and draper in Staithes, a fishing village nearby. He remained there for eighteen months before leaving this employment, with his master's agreement, and entering the service, as an apprentice, of John Walker, a quaker shipowner of Whitby. The sea became his chosen career and from 1746 to 1755 he advanced from apprentice to mate, and almost to master, in a number of ships in the east coast and North Sea coal trade based at Whitby [5]. During this time he learnt much of the seamanship which stood him in good stead later, such as the intricacies of navigation in awkward coastal waters and the handling of the vessel peculiar to the Whitby coal trade, the cat-built collier. It was to be the vessel chosen for all three of his voyages of exploration, with a characteristic blunt bow and broad belly. In 1755 Cook took a curious step; he turned down the offer of a command by Walker and, instead, volunteered for the Royal Navy as an able-seaman. In normal circumstances, there was nothing in conditions below decks in the Royal Navy of the period (deeply engaged as it was, in the Seven Years' War with France) to entice a promising young sailor in the merchant marine to transfer from the one to the other, losing rank and status as he did so, and biographers have hitherto been at something of a loss to explain Cook's motive. However, there has been a recent suggestion that Cook, in addition to plying legitimate trade, also indulged in smuggling and had the misfortune to be discovered. Whatever may be the truth of this assertion (it is not difficult to imagine a situation where Cook might have had to take responsibility for the illicit activities of one or more members of his crew), the avoidance of the unpleasant legal

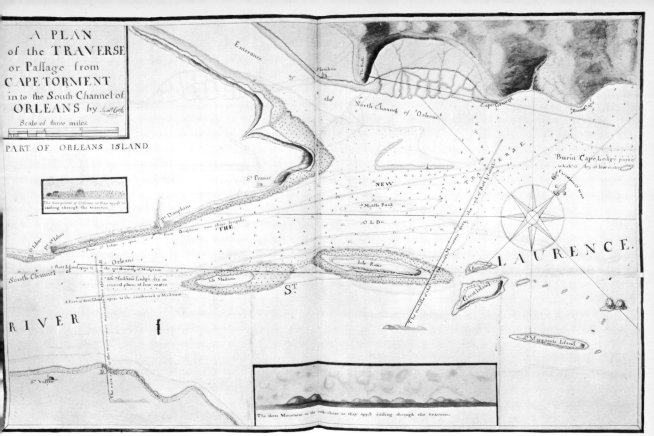

A PLAN of the TRAVERSE or Paſſage from CAPE TORMENT in to the South Channel of ORLEANS by Iamᵈ Cook

Scale of three miles

6 Cook's chart of the navigable channel in the St Lawrence River downstream from Quebec, 1759. The chart of the channel was essential to enable Wolfe to capture Quebec. *Add. MS 31360 f.14*

consequences of such a predicament provides a better motive for what was a critical turning point in his career than has so far been adduced.

He served in a succession of ships, and such was his experience and ability that he received relatively rapid advancement to master. Of his commanders, Hugh Palliser, his second, was to be a staunch ally for the rest of his life. The spring of 1759 found Cook, as master of the *Pembroke*, in the St Lawrence River charting a notorious zig-zag, known as the Traverse, in the channel of the river as it approached Quebec. This was to enable Wolfe's expedition to attack the city held by the French [6]. His brief participation in this event of great strategic significance was followed by some years spent surveying first the St Lawrence and then parts of Nova Scotia. Cook had shown an especial aptitude for survey work and, at the cessation of hostilities, surveyed the coasts of Newfoundland, eventually, as a warrant officer, commanding his own vessel, the schooner *Grenville*. The Newfoundland survey lasted five years and began with a rapid survey of the islands of St Pierre and Miquelon, made in a great hurry for strategic reasons before they were returned to the French under the provisions of the Treaty of Paris [7]. His superior for much of the later time spent on the survey was Hugh Palliser, now the Governor of Newfoundland. Such was the quality of Cook's work (the charts he drew were eventually published in the *North*

Scale of Feet

ROAD

References

A Stages to Split and Salt fish in
B Wharf
C Beach for drying fish on
D Rocks above Water
+ Rocks under Water

The Figures shew the depth of Water in
fathoms at low water.

The Tide Flows full and change

Pigeon Island   Cartload Rocks

Sheep Rocks

Boar Island

Great Black Rocks

Little Black Rocks

Harbour Rock

7 A rough chart of the harbour of St Pierre by Cook, 1763. The islands of St Pierre and Miquelon were returned to the French after the Seven Years War, but not until Cook had completed a survey of them. *Add. MS 31360 f.20*

8 The *Endeavour* at sea, sketch by Sydney Parkinson, (?) 1768. *Add. MS 9345 f.16v*

American Pilot and remained unsuperseded for nearly a century), and such was Palliser's influence, that when a commander for the new voyage to the South Pacific was sought in the autumn of 1767, the little-known Cook was chosen for the task. He was now thirty-nine and the father of three (he had married Elizabeth Batts of Barking on a visit home in December 1762), and in twelve years in the Royal Navy he had risen from able-seaman to a lieutenant's commission.

The actual aim of the intended voyage was the discovery of the Great Southern Continent, but ostensibly the published intention was to convey to a suitable point in the South Pacific a Royal Society team to observe the transit of Venus across the face of the sun on 3 June 1769. It was thought that calculations based on the differentials between the transit time as observed in widely differing parts of the world would determine the distance of the earth from the sun and from Venus. It was, however, essential that one of the observation points should be in the South Pacific, and the Royal Society, much exercised in the matter, petitioned the King for funds to send an expedition there for the purpose. On being promised the necessary support, the Society appointed Alexander Dalrymple to be its observer. He was eager to go; but his eagerness stemmed rather from the opportunity of going to find his continent than from any astronomical zeal, and when it was made clear to him that he would not be in command of the ship which transported the team to the Pacific he withdrew from the plan.

The ship which Cook was to command was the *Earl of Pembroke*, a cat-built Whitby collier rechristened the *Endeavour* [8], and stores were provided for a two-year voyage. The timely return of Wallis in the *Dolphin* provided some crew with

9 Alexander Buchan, an undated self-portrait. Buchan was employed by Banks to draw views on the first voyage, but died soon after arriving at Tahiti. *Reproduced by courtesy of the owner, Professor C.M.D. Crowder.*

10 View of 'One-Tree Hill' with Matavai Bay and Cook's encampment at Fort Venus in the background, by Sydney Parkinson, 1769. *Add. MS 23921 f.6*

experience of the Pacific and, more important, the precise location of an island, Tahiti, which would be an ideal observation point. The Royal Society named as its observers Charles Green and Cook himself, and, in addition, asked if one of its Fellows, the young Joseph Banks, might join the ship's company with a retinue of seven. This was to include two paid artists, Alexander Buchan [9] and Sydney Parkinson, to draw views and natural history specimens, a secretary (also a trained draughtsman) and, in particular, his friend, Daniel Carl Solander, the naturalist and pupil of Linnaeus [50]. It was thus due to Banks's initiative and youthful enthusiasm that, almost by accident, this voyage of exploration was the first to be adequately equipped to assess and record whatever might be encountered in the sphere of natural science. 'No people ever went to sea better fitted to the purpose of Natural History' wrote the natural historian, John Ellis, to Linnaeus (Beaglehole, 1955, cxxxvi). Banks had, at the age of twenty-one, succeeded to his family estates in Lincolnshire, and was now, aged twenty-five, in a financial position to indulge a passion for botany and zoology to a degree quite remarkable for the times. Two years before he had made extensive collections of plants and animals in Newfoundland (possibly meeting Cook there) and he now eagerly grasped this immense opportunity.

Cook's formal instructions were signed by the Lords of the Admiralty on 30 July 1768: he was to proceed around Cape Horn and so to Tahiti to carry out the observation; he was to treat the natives with friendship, but also with caution. There were additional secret instructions: after the transit he was to sail south to latitude 40° in search of the Great Southern Continent and, if he had not encountered it by then, he was to sail west until he either discovered it in that direction or else made landfall on the east coast of New Zealand. He was to explore and chart as much of New Zealand's coast as might be practicable in the circumstances and then return home. The *Endeavour* sailed from Plymouth on 26 August 1768 and the voyage proceeded smoothly according to plan; Madeira and Rio de Janeiro were ports of call on the way south and by January 1769 they were off Tierra del Fuego, where they put in at the 'Bay of Good Success'. On 13 April Cook dropped anchor at Matavai Bay, Tahiti [10].

The details of their meetings with the peoples of Tahiti and of Oceania in general, both on this and the two subsequent voyages are discussed in later chapters. At present we are concerned with the bare outline of the voyages, the framework, as it were, within which the encounters took place. The *Endeavour* remained at Tahiti for some six weeks; the island was surveyed [11], the transit of Venus was duly observed (unfortunately, the grand world-wide operation was a failure because a penumbra, or shadow, around the planet made accurate measurement virtually impossible, though this only emerged later), and Cook put into effect the secret part of his instructions. He set sail on 13 July 1769, heading south and then, finding no trace of the continent north of latitude 39°, turned west and, on 7 October, the east coast of the North Island of New Zealand came into sight [12]. In the short space of five and a half months he circumnavigated both islands starting on a northern course

11 Chart of Tahiti by Cook, 1769. Compare this with the crude effort of George Pinnock made two years earlier (4), and one can get an impression of Cook's expertise as a surveyor. South is at the top of the page. *Add. MS 7085 f.6*

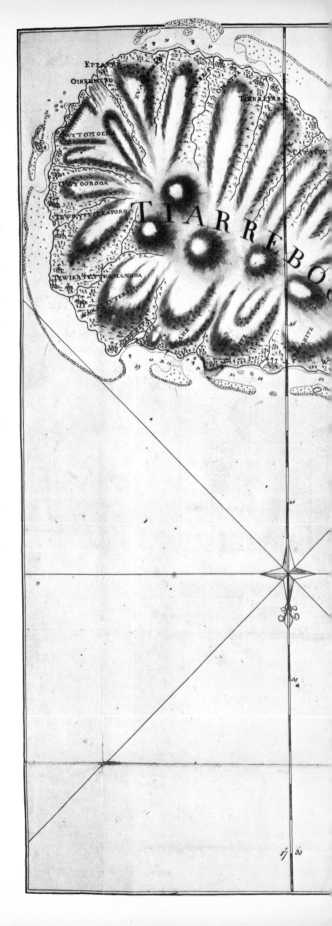

A Plan of King Georges Island or Otaheite

By Lieutenant J. Cook 1769 Discover'd by Capt. Wallis the 19th June 1767.

A SCALE of MILES

O P O O R E O N O O

12 Tolaga Bay, New Zealand, with sailors handling water-casks. A drawing apparentl

Cook based on an original drawing by Hermann Spöring, 1769. *Add. MS 7085 f.21*

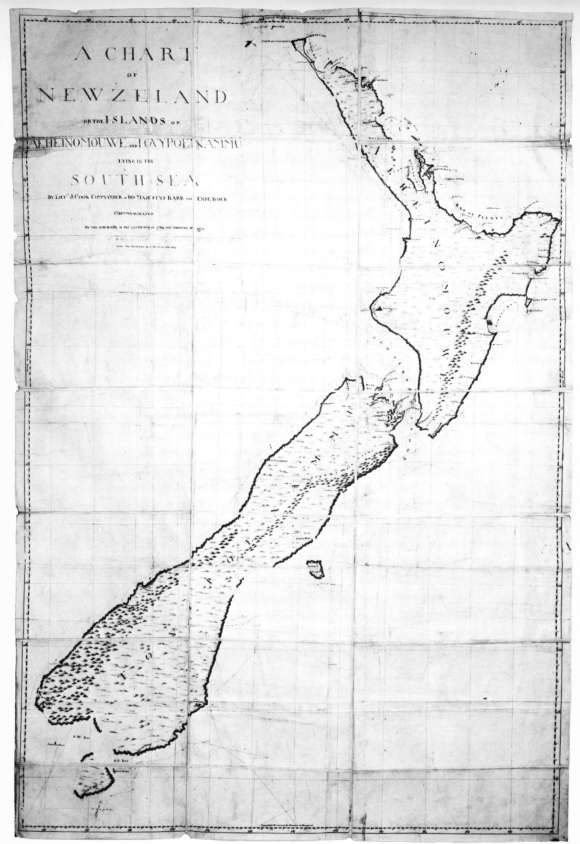

13 Chart of New Zealand by Cook, 1770. Cook charted the coast of New Zealand, hitherto thought to be part of the Great Southern Continent, in a bare five and a half months. There is an error in longitude, while Banks Peninsula is thought to be an island, and Stewart Island is thought to be a peninsula. *Add. MS 7085 f.16*

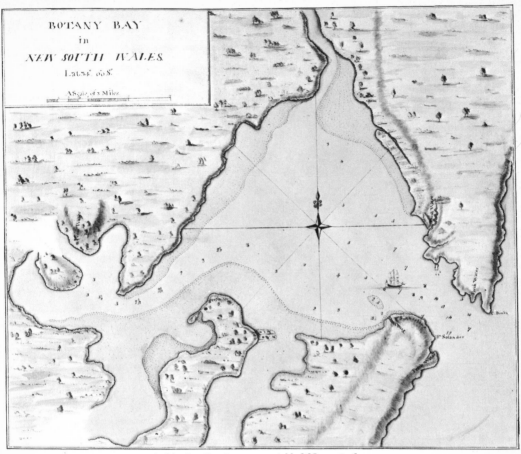

14 Chart of Botany Bay, probably by Cook, 1770. *Add. MS 31360 f.32*

and was able to draw a chart of extraordinary accuracy [13] which disproved the notion that New Zealand was any part of the continent. Taking possession of the country for the King and having fulfilled his instructions, he used his discretion to sail west towards the presumed east coast of New Holland, which had not previously been visited by Europeans, though the outline of the west and south coasts was well charted. The coast was sighted on 19 April and was duly charted from the point of encounter (Point Hicks) north to Cape York. Calls were made at Botany Bay [14], so called because of the large number of plants collected there by Banks and Solander, and at Endeavour River, where, because of having gone seriously aground on the Great Barrier Reef, much time had to be spent on repairs. (To refloat and plug the hole in the hull had demanded all the skill in seamanship Cook possessed.) They reached Batavia in Java in October and left it at the end of December, reaching England by way of Cape Town in July, 1770.

[33]

In London, the public was impatient to hear of the voyage. Cook had sent a copy of his journal, some charts and a brief report on ahead by a ship leaving Batavia soon after his arrival there so that the outline of his achievements was known. Partly because of their respective stations in life, and partly because of his spectacular collections, the public acclaimed Banks as the hero of the voyage, rather than Cook; he had, with Solander, collected a mass of specimens, ethnographical, botanical and zoological, and there were many drawings by his artists, Buchan, Parkinson and Spöring. Everyone clamoured to see them. If less public notice was taken of Cook, the Admiralty were not slow to express their satisfaction with the voyage, he was promoted Commander, and the King granted him an audience. Cook summed up the voyage in a letter to his old master in Whitby, John Walker: 'I have made no very great Discoveries yet I exploar'd more of the Great South Sea than all that have gone before me so much that little remains now to be done to have a thorough knowledge of that part of the Globe' (Beaglehole, 1974, 276).

Certainly Cook had not discovered the continent, nor had he covered quite enough of the southern Pacific to rule out the existence of the continent, although its location would now need to be in more southerly latitudes than had previously been supposed. Indeed, he was so aware of this lingering possibility that he put forward a plan to the Admiralty for a second voyage to pursue the continent as far south as might be necessary. He had arrived home in July, and by September plans were being laid for a second voyage, in two ships. Cook's status, enhanced by the favour of the Earl of Sandwich, First Sea Lord, and the influence of his old friend, Captain Palliser, now head of the Navy Board and as such controller of supplies, enabled him to requisition all that he needed. The two ships were, again, Whitby colliers, bought and renamed *Resolution* [15] and *Adventure*.

Banks of course was eager to join this second voyage and sail to the South Seas again; he rather expected the voyage to be run according to his directions and, on being invited to go, insisted that an extra upper deck be added to the *Resolution* to accommodate his suite, this time to comprise no less than thirteen persons. This superstructure had to be quickly removed because it made the vessel hopelessly ungainly and top-heavy. At this, Banks withdrew from the enterprise in fury. However the Admiralty appointed an official artist to the ship's company, William Hodges, and there was also to be a naturalist, Johann Reinhold Forster, and an astronomer, William Wales. The second ship, the *Adventure*, was commanded by Tobias Furneaux. It says much for Cook that a number of the *Endeavour*'s crew signed on for the second voyage, including Charles Clerke and Richard Pickersgill (master's mate on the *Endeavour*, and now third lieutenant).

They sailed from Plymouth on 27 June 1772 directly south by Cape Town. By December they were amongst icebergs and in January 1773 the Antarctic Circle was

15 The *Resolution*, Cook's ship on the second and third voyages, drawn by John Webber. *Add. MS 17277 f.1*

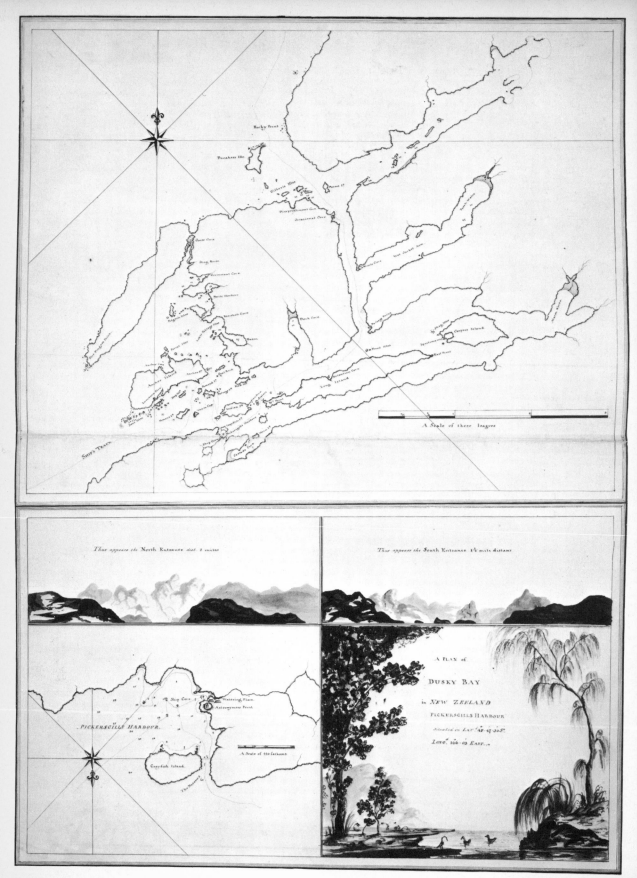

16 Chart and coastal views of Dusky Bay, South Island, New Zealand by Henry Roberts, 1773. *Add. MS 31360 f.55*

17 Detail from a view of Tahiti, with canoes, by William Hodges, probably 1773.
Add. MS 15743 f.9

crossed for the first time; further progress was blocked by pack-ice. Cook retreated
north and, in February, lost contact with the *Adventure* in a fog. This possibility had
been foreseen and there was a plan to rendezvous in New Zealand if necessary. Cook
proceeded there by as southernly a route as was practicable in order to stand the best
chance of finding the continent. He reached New Zealand in March and put into
Dusky Bay on the south-west of South Island [16]. After a stay of some six weeks to
recuperate and refit after the rigours of the Antarctic, he sailed north to Queen
Charlotte Sound where he duly found the *Adventure*. Further exploration to the
south was out of the question for the time being, since it was the southern winter,
and so Cook made his second visit to Tahiti [17], staying for just over a fortnight
before sailing in search of some islands known from Tasman's voyage in 1643. These
were the Tongan group, which Cook named the Friendly Islands because of the
extremely good relations he was able to establish with the inhabitants. At Tahiti, he
had taken on board the *Resolution* a native named Hiti-Hiti (called by the crew
Odiddy), while Furneaux had taken on board a Raiatean named Omai (British
Museum, 1979, 81 ff.)

18 Resolution Harbour, Marquesas
Islands, by William Hodges, 1774.
Add. MS 15743 f.4

19 Head-dress of pearl-shell with turtle-
shell overlay and feathers from the
Marquesas Islands, *l.42 cm. Pitt Rivers
Museum, Oxford. Forster Collection no.134*

Towards the end of winter (in October) they returned to New Zealand before making a further foray to the Antarctic. Unfortunately, just before reaching Queen Charlotte Sound, the ships once again lost contact with each other in a storm, and this time they did not succeed in joining up. Furneaux made for home more or less directly and arrived there a full year before Cook. Cook, for his part, penetrated the Antarctic Circle twice during the course of the next two months, reaching a point within 1300 miles of the South Pole before ice made further progress dangerous. At last Cook gave up the idea that the Great Southern Continent existed in any form other than as the frozen land mass we know as Antarctica; the grandiose theories of Dalrymple and his forerunners were finally demolished. Cook wrote in his journal: 'I whose ambition leads me not only further than any other man has been before me, but as far as I think it possible for man to go, was not sorry at meeting with this interruption . . .' (Beaglehole, 1961, 322).

This was the climax of the second voyage; thereafter he returned north to Tahiti for a second winter by way of Easter Island (reached on 12 March; here the weird stone statues were a cause of wonder) and the Marquesas Islands [18, 19]. Hiti-Hiti was returned to his home, and after a short stay, Cook pressed on to explore what are

20 Chart of the track of the second voyage, apparently by Cook, *c.*1775. *Add. MS 31360 f.7*

now called the New Hebrides and the island of New Caledonia. By the later part of October he was back in New Zealand at Queen Charlotte Sound (the third visit on this voyage) and ready to head for home eastwards across the Pacific, past Cape Horn and on across the Atlantic, all roughly in the same latitude of 60° south. In this way he had circumnavigated the globe at that latitude and shown that there could be no continent there. On crossing his original track south of some two years before, he turned north to Cape Town, called there, and reached home in July after a voyage of just over three years [20].

Much the same London pattern repeated itself: there was an audience with the King, he was promoted Captain and elected a Fellow of the Royal Society. He received full recognition as a great navigator and was placed on the establishment of Greenwich Hospital in order to preserve his active service pay. It was generally expected that he would now retire.

Omai, the Polynesian from Raiatea brought home by Furneaux was a great curiosity and sought after as a guest at fashionable dinner parties. But his success as a social phenomenon could not go on for ever and the need to return him home was the pretext for a third voyage on which the *Resolution* would be accompanied by another ship, the *Discovery*. The benefit of Cook's experience and advice was much in demand while the ships were being fitted out although he was not expected to take command. He had made his contribution and little more could be asked of him, but Cook volunteered, and the Admiralty accepted his offer with alacrity. It is likely that Cook found the comparative inactivity of London life insupportable after so many years spent in the wide spaces of the Pacific.

The excuse for the voyage was the return of Omai, but the stimulus was provided by that other great geographical chimaera, the North-West Passage. The Great Southern Continent had been disposed of but the Passage remained. The discovery by Bering of the strait called after him lent an air of probability to the existence of such a passage somewhere north of the strait and south of the region of Baffin Bay. The plan was to send Pickersgill, Cook's lieutenant on the second voyage, to find the eastern approach, while Cook would search for the western. Charles Clerke was given command of the *Discovery* and amongst the crews were two future navigators of note, William Bligh and George Vancouver. Once again there was an official artist, John Webber, to be assisted by the surgeon's mate, William Ellis. The surgeon, William Anderson, was also responsible for most of the botanical and ethnographical observations.

The ships sailed separately at the height of summer 1776 (the *Discovery* in July and the *Resolution* in August) on a fairly direct route to New Zealand, calling at Cape Town (where they joined up), the wild and barren Kerguelen Island in the southern Indian Ocean [Plate 11], the coast of Van Diemen's Land (Tasmania), and they

reached Queen Charlotte Sound on 12 February 1777. The onward leg to Tahiti was frustrated by contrary winds, so Cook revisited the Friendly Islands where he spent twelve weeks, until 17 July [21, 22]. Four weeks later the ships were at Tahiti for Cook's fourth and final visit. Omai was returned to Huahine (the ships' carpenters built him a house) and on 7 December the two ships set course for the north, with the northern summer before them to search for the Passage.

On 18 January 1778 Cook unexpectedly discovered the Hawaiian islands; he had not expected to find Polynesian settlement so far north. On a visit which lasted barely a fortnight he only saw the outlying islands of Kauai and Niihau, not the main island of the group, Hawaii itself. The summer was approaching and he could not delay; he pressed on towards the coast of 'New Albion', as Drake had christened the north-west coast of America. It took five weeks to sight it at a point in modern Oregon, but they did not find an anchorage until they reached Nootka Sound on the west coast of Vancouver Island. Here a long stay of some four weeks was necessary to repair damage to the *Resolution*, which needed a new mizzen mast and was leaking badly. Proceeding north along the mountainous coast to Alaska they found another

21 Dance performed
before Cook at night
by women of the
Ha'apai Islands,
Tonga, engraved after
a drawing by John
Webber, 1777.
Add. MS 23920 f.99

22 Wood bucket from
Tonga, covered with
basketry and decorated
with shell and
coconut-shell beads.
h. 43.5 cm. NN

23 *Resolution* and *Discovery* in Prince William Sound, Alaska, by John Webber, 1778. *Add. MS 15514 f.8*

anchorage in Prince William Sound [23] and again at one of the Aleutian islands, Unalaska. A northward course took them through the Bering Strait in early August and into the Arctic Ocean, where they hoped to find the North-West Passage. Probings in various directions were inevitably blocked by ice and the onset of winter necessitated a return first to Unalaska for further repairs to the *Resolution* and then on to Hawaii, reached on 26 November 1778. A suitable anchorage was found at Kealakekua Bay on 16 January 1779 where the ships remained until 4 February. Relations with the Hawaiians were good and the stay was pleasant.

The plan was to leave Hawaii for the Russian coast at Kamchatka and from there, with the arrival of summer, it would be easy to approach the Bering Strait once again in search of the Passage. Unfortunately, four days out from Hawaii, a storm damaged the *Resolution*'s foremast and Cook decided to return to Kealakekua Bay for repairs [24]. The story of how Cook came to be murdered there is told in a later chapter. His place on the *Resolution* was taken by Charles Clerke who, determining to fulfil Cook's plan of action, sailed to Kamchatka, and again through the Bering Sea to the Arctic Ocean. Ice frustrated the venture as in the year before, and returning to Kamchatka, he died of tuberculosis. The ships, now commanded by Gore and King, proceeded along the coast of China, through the East Indies, across the Indian Ocean to Cape Town and so home. Bad weather drove them to the Orkney Islands and it was October 1780 before they finally anchored in the Nore.

Cook had kept a daily journal throughout all three voyages, and so had many of his companions, thus there is a greater wealth of detail available than for any previous exploration. Banks had introduced the concept of including in the company trained artists and scientists to collect and record; every aspect of the travellers' experience was noted and assessed since all were fully aware of the importance of the enterprise. Therefore there existed a corpus of writings, drawings, paintings, artefacts and natural history specimens which provided abundant raw material for what was the prime task following each voyage: the satisfaction of the public clamour for information about the amazing new discoveries.

24 The *Discovery* in rough weather, by John Webber, (?) 1778. This sketch was presumably taken from the *Resolution* and shows signs of what may be sea-spray. *Add. MS 17277 f.5*

The original records of the voyages, the journals, objects and drawings, were jealously preserved by those who owned them: Banks, the Admiralty, Cook's widow and others. Banks left his collection to the British Museum, founded in 1753 for the particular purpose of preserving such things, and the collection formed a magnet which attracted many additions. This collection was divided between the appropriate Departments: objects to the Department of Ethnography, drawings and journals to the Department of Manuscripts and so on. Because of the subsequent growth and internal division of the Museum, the collection is now housed in three institutions (the British Museum (Natural History), the Museum of Mankind, and the British Library), but as a whole it forms the basis of the present exhibition. Although the British Museum and British Library collections may form the core of the original records of the voyages, many separate items, some of signal importance, are to be found elsewhere in locations as far apart as Sydney, Vienna, Vancouver and Hawaii.

2 The Society Islands

DOROTA CZARKOWSKA STARZECKA

COOK was not the first European to visit the Society Islands. They were discovered by Captain Samuel Wallis of HMS *Dolphin* who landed on Tahiti in 1767. In 1768 the Frenchman Louis de Bougainville in *La Boudeuse* called there and – impressed by the island's beauty – gave it another name, New Cythera, after the Peloponnesian island where the goddess Aphrodite first emerged from the sea. Cook was, however, the first European to spend any considerable time in the islands (he visited them on each of his three voyages, and twice on the second); he was thus in a position to give the first reliable account of them and of their people. He gave the islands the name which they bear today – Society Islands, '. . . as they lay contiguous to one a nother . . .' (Beaglehole, 1955, 151).

The islands lie between the Equator and the Tropic of Capricorn, but nearer the latter, and divide naturally into two groups, the Windward group to the east, the principal islands of which are Tahiti and Moorea, and the Leeward group to the west, the main islands being Huahine, Raiatea and Borabora. The larger islands are high and rugged, of volcanic origin, with sharp peaks, precipitous cliffs and deep valleys. They are well-watered, the soil on the coast is very fertile, and the vegetation lush. Because of the trade winds the climate, although hot and humid, is not oppressive. The islands are very beautiful [Plate III]. With their continuous summer, spectacular mountains, abundance of fruit and flowers, coconut groves and beaches and the dazzlingly blue sea around, they are everything that the evocative phrase 'South Sea islands' implies.

In Cook's time they were inhabited by about 70,000 Polynesians, a well-built, attractive people, whose skin varied from almost fair to brown, whose hair was black, sometimes wavy, and eyes large and dark: 'their features are agreable and their gate gracefull' wrote Cook (*ibid.*, 124). Their ultimate place of origin, a question which intrigued Cook, is today thought to be in Asia, somewhere around the South China Sea. We also now know that they had already settled in these islands by about AD 860, perhaps even as early as AD 650, and that they probably arrived from the

25 Stylised image of a god made of wood and coconut fibre. Society Islands. *l.* 61.5 cm. *TAH 64*

Marquesas or possibly from Samoa. Long before Captain Cook appeared in this area, the Polynesians colonised all the islands of the eastern, and some of the western half of the Pacific. Cook was to encounter them repeatedly during his voyages, in islands scattered over the vast stretches of the sea, and was puzzled and impressed by them: 'How shall we account for this Nation spreading it self so far over this Vast ocean? We find them from New Zealand to the South, to these islands to the North [Hawaii] and from Easter Island to the Hebrides [the New Hebrides]' (Beaglehole, 1967, 279). On his third voyage he met in Atiu, one of the Cook Islands, four Tahitians, whose canoe had drifted there during a voyage from Tahiti to Raiatea. Here he thought he had found the answer: 'This circumstance very well accounts for the manner the inhabited islands in this Sea have been at first peopled; especially those which lay remote from any Continent and from each other' (*ibid.*, 87). Though widely scattered, they spoke the same language, had the same basic religious beliefs, and the way their society was organised arose from these religious beliefs.

The Tahitians (which for convenience the Society Islanders will be called here) believed that the universe was created by the god Ta'aroa. Ta'aroa also created other gods, *atua*, among whom the most important were Tu, Tane and 'Oro. Tane was considered to be the nearest to Ta'aroa (sometimes he was also considered to be the first man); Tu was the god of craftsmen and it was with his help that Ta'aroa created man; 'Oro was god of war and towards the end of the eighteenth century his cult was achieving its greatest prominence. 'Oro had his own special following in the *Arioi*, a religious society of players and musicians who travelled among the islands, spreading 'Oro's fame. *Atua* could manifest themselves in *ata* – natural beings or objects (birds, clouds, etc.) or in *to'o* – manufactured images, sometimes quite abstract in form, sometimes with certain anthropomorphic features [25]. An indispensable adjunct of these images were red and yellow feathers, and when such images were transported from one place to another they were placed in specially built god-houses [26] on consecrated canoes. Besides the *atua* there was another

26 House in which the image shown in (27) was kept. Society Islands. *l.* 87.5 cm *LMS 120. Not from Cook's voyages*

27 Image of a minor
   female deity,
   originally kept in
   the god-house
   shown in (26).
   Society Islands
   h. 10.5 cm. LMS 98.
   *Not from Cook's
   voyages*

28 Wood image,
   probably of a minor
   deity. This figure
   was found inside
   the mourner's dress
   (Plate VI) (used as a
   support for the
   headpiece) when it
   was dismantled for
   cleaning and repairs
   in 1966. Society
   Islands. *h.* 46.5 cm.
   TAH 78a

category of spirits – '*oromatua*. These were ghosts, souls of the dead. They were less powerful than the *atua* but concerned themselves more with the everyday affairs of the people. When their power was harnessed by sorcerers, they were invoked to enter small images called *ti'i* [27, 28].

[49]

29 *(overleaf)* Cook observing a ceremony
   involving human sacrifice on Tahiti,
   1 September 1777, by John Webber.
   Add. MS 15513 f.16

Gods were worshipped in open-air temples called *marae* which were enclosed areas with stone structures, surrounded by trees especially associated with *marae* (ironwoods, rosewoods); an important feature was a stone platform, *ahu*, the resting place for the gods. *Marae* varied greatly in importance and elaboration, from simple ones, which every family possessed and where the head of the family worshipped, to the imposing tribal and international *marae*, with a large body of priests and attendants, where the high chiefs worshipped. Priests in general were called *tahu'a pure*, specialists in praying, and those holding positions in important *marae* were trained in special schools. The usual offerings to the gods were foodstuffs though human sacrifices were performed at the most venerated *marae*, mainly those dedicated to 'Oro, to mark significant occasions in the life of the supreme chief and events of national importance like war. Captain Cook witnessed such a ceremony with a human sacrifice during his last stay in the Society Islands [29].

The complete system of religious ideas in the Society Islands was extremely complex, and only a few basic elements can be indicated here. The essential underlying principle of the Tahitian view of life and universe, and of the interaction between gods and humans, was the dual concept of the sacred and the profane. Gods, and people and objects associated with them, were sacred – *mo'a* or *ra'a*; anybody or anything devoid of this sacredness was profane – *noa*. Sacredness was considered to be dangerous, and any entity imbued with more sacredness was dangerous to any with less; the former therefore was *tapu* – prohibited, restricted, set outside normal contact or use. Interaction between the gods and human beings was based on the principle of reciprocal obligation: the gods had definite obligations towards men in exchange for the worship and offerings they received. If these obligations were not fulfilled, the images of the gods could be discarded and replaced by others.

Religious dogma lay at the foundations of social organisation. There were three social classes. The highest were the *ari'i* – the aristocracy, the chiefs. Among them those of the highest rank were the *ari'i maro-'ura*, the only chiefs who had the right to wear the red feather girdle (*maro-'ura*), which was supposed to be the garment of the gods. The *ra'atira* were the middle class, owing allegiance to the *ari'i* and exercising direct control over the lowest class, the commoners – the *manahune* – who cultivated the land and provided various services to the two upper classes. The position of an individual in society depended on his descent and his genealogy justified his social rank, which meant, in practical terms, that the elder sibling ranked above the younger, and the descendants of the older above the descendants of the younger, and the male line of descent was preferred to the female (women, with the exception of the highly born, were considered *noa* – profane). The highest chiefs claimed direct descent from the gods and were sacred. Everything which came into contact with

30 Basketry and feather head-dress
(*fau*) worn with a feather breast
gorget (Plate IV). Society Islands.
h. 162.5 cm. *TAH 9*

them became sacred, too. When they moved out of their domain, they had to be carried by retainers, to prevent the ground on which they might walk from becoming *tapu*. Any infringement of a chief's *tapu* was an offence, often punishable by death. They had complete political power over their territories (tribal districts of varying extent and complexity) which they administered with the help of minor chiefs. Ideally, political power coincided with genealogical pre-eminence but sometimes the highest-ranking chief was ineffective, and political authority was exercised by a lower-ranking one of greater ability. In general, lower-ranking chiefs and *ra'atira* played an important political role both in supporting and checking the power of the highest chiefs.

In a society where all the land was divided among chiefs competing for territory and prestige, war was inevitably frequent. Before a chief decided to embark upon it, he sought the advice of the priests and minor chiefs, consulted oracles and, once the decision was made, religious ceremonies, lasting three days and involving human sacrifice to ensure a favourable outcome, were performed at the *marae*. Battles were fought on land and sea with spears, clubs, daggers and slings. For armour mats and sennit cords were wound tightly round body and limbs while important men wore gorgets, breast coverings made of feathers, shark teeth, shell and dog hair on a basketry base [Plate IV], and imposing head-dresses, *fau*, which were basketry cylinders decorated with feathers [**30**]. Naval battles were usually more important

[53]

and decisive than those fought on land. Their war canoes [31] were twin-hulled vessels, with high stems and a fighting platform built across the hulls over the bow, which were propelled by paddlers sitting behind and underneath the platform. Cook saw a Tahitian armada being made ready for war against the island of Moorea during his second voyage: 'we took our time to view this fleet, the Vessels of War consisted of 160 large double Canoes, very well equip'd, Man'd and Arm'd . . . The Cheifs ie all those on the Fighting Stages were drist in their War habits . . . they were complesant enough to Shew themselves to the best advantage, their Vessels were decorated with Flags, Streamers etc. so that the whole made a grand and Noble appearence' (Beaglehole, 1961, 385).

31 A Tahitian war canoe, by Sydney Parkinson, 1769. Notice the breast gorgets (Plate IV) and the *fau* (30) and the man bailing. *Add. MS 23921 f.21*

32 View in Vaitepiha Bay, Tahiti, by John Webber, 1777. *Add. MS 15513 f.13*

Cook and his men never saw a Tahitian battle. If they had, it would certainly have altered their rather rosy view of the islands, for they were fought with great ferocity and savagery. The vanquished were pursued and cut down without mercy and with great cruelty. Women and children were slaughtered, lands laid to waste and *marae* desecrated and when it was all over, the victors celebrated with feasts and thanksgiving ceremonies at their *marae*, while the vanquished performed ceremonies to purify the land and restore the sanctity of their *marae*.

Everyday life was easy, and to European eyes almost like paradise. They lived not in villages but in scattered homesteads connected by well-kept, shady walks. Houses were wood-framed structures, thatched with coconut or pandanus leaves, usually without walls, excellently suited to the climate [32]. They also had small portable

33 A Tahitian canoe with a portable house on the platform, by John Webber, 1777. *Add. MS 15513 f.25*

34 A canoe shed on Raiatea ('Ulietea'), by Sydney Parkinson, 1769. *Add. MS 23921 f.11*

35 Wood headrest. Society Islands. *l.* 24.5 cm. *TAH 1*

houses which could be placed on a canoe platform or used on land when travelling [33]. There were special cook-houses and sheds for canoes [34], very rough-and-ready structures. The furnishings were very simple: mats to sit and sleep on, wood headrests used as pillows [35] and wooden stools. Weapons, tools [36] and clothing were suspended from the rafters and beams, or from a special rack inside or just outside the house. As pottery and metals were unknown, domestic utensils consisted

36 Stone-bladed adze with vegetable-fibre lashing.
Society Islands. *l.* 61 cm. *TAH 88*

[57]

of wood dishes [37], sometimes with four legs, stone pounders [38] used with wood pounding tables, gourd water bottles and coconut cups. Musical instruments [39], except for the large temple drums, were also kept in the house.

The basis of subsistence was farming and fishing. The favourable climate and the fertility of the soil meant that farming did not require great skills or expenditure of time. The staple food was breadfruit, usually baked in an earth oven using heated stones. Other cultivated plants were taro, sweet potato, yams, sugar cane, paper mulberry for manufacture of barkcloth, and a shrub of the pepper family for making

37 (*above*) Wood food bowl. Society Islands. *l.* 79.5 cm. *TAH 4*

38 (*top right*) Stone food pounder. Society Islands. *h.* 18.5 cm. *TAH 15*

39 Wood drum with sharkskin membrane and coconut-fibre lashing. Society Islands. *h.* 63.5 cm. *TAH 22*

40 Tahitian canoes engraved after a drawing by Sydney Parkinson, 1769. *Hawkesworth, 1773, plate 4*

kava, a mildly narcotic beverage which was prepared from the root of the plant by chewing it and infusing the pulp with water. There were also various wild fruits and, of course, the versatile coconut.

The only domesticated animals were 'Hogs Fowls and Dogs the latter of which we learned to eat from them and few were there of us but what allowe'd that a South Sea Dog was next to an English Lamb', wrote Cook (Beaglehole, 1955, 121–2). Fishing was a skilled occupation, using outrigger canoes with a sail or paddled [40] and the Tahitians were particularly expert in making nets, both simple hand-scoop ones and large seines. They caught fish with hook-and-line both in the lagoons and the open sea, the hooks being made of wood, shell and bone, and also by spearing, trapping and stupefying them with vegetable drugs. Part of the necessary equipment of a canoe was a bailer [41].

41 Canoe bailer. Society Islands. *l.* 45.5 cm.
    TAH 6

42 Wooden barkcloth beater.
Society Islands. *l.* 38 cm. *TAH 20*

Farming, fishing, and canoe building were male occupations, but women joined in some activities, like helping in cultivation or collecting shellfish. Men also made cordage out of coconut husk fibre and the bark of the hibiscus tree, though mats and baskets were usually made by women, and barkcloth manufacture was a totally female sphere of activity. The cloth was made from the inner bark of the paper mulberry or the breadfruit tree, soaked in water and beaten on a flat board with a wood beater [42] into thin strips, which were later felted together to produce large sheets of cloth.

Clothing consisted of a loincloth (*maro*) for men, a short underskirt (*pareu*) for women, over which both sexes wore a wrap-around (also *pareu*) – from waist to knees for males, and from above the breasts to below the knees for women. Over this a poncho-like garment could be worn, and women sometimes wore in addition a large cloak. These garments could not be washed, and were therefore replaced frequently. Cook wrote: 'They are a very cleanly people both in their persons and diat always washing their hands and mouth immidiatly before and after their meals and wash or bathe themselves in fresh water three times a day' (*ibid.*, 124). Their only unpleasing habit was the custom of oiling their hair; the oil, when rancid, made 'the wearer of it smell not very agreable' (*ibid.*, 124). They placed a high value on physical attractiveness and spent much time and effort on grooming; their personal ornaments were few, mainly earrings, worn in one ear, of shell, seeds or pearls, and flowers in the hair [43]. They also tattooed their bodies by dipping a bone implement

43 Young woman of Tahiti with two gorgets, by John Webber, 1777. *Add. MS 15513 f.17* (See also Plate IV)

in candlenut soot, placing it on the skin and tapping it with a wooden mallet [44, 45] to produce a design. Some of Cook's men tried it, among them Sydney Parkinson, the draughtsman on the *Endeavour*: 'Mr Stainsby, myself, and some others of our company, underwent the operation, and had our arms marked' (Parkinson, 1773, 25). Fatness and white skin were considered beautiful, and many people, especially the young, spent long periods sheltered from the sun, inactive and consuming enormous amounts of fattening food. In fact, to European eyes, the Tahitians seemed to spend a lot of time in idleness; 'After their meals and in the heat of the day they often sleep middle aged people especialy, the better sort of whom seem to spend most of their time in eating and sleeping' (Beaglehole, 1955, 126). Most of the work was done in the morning, and after the main meal of the day in the early afternoon, and a siesta, the rest of the time was spent chatting, visiting, in sports like swimming, surfing, wrestling and boxing. There were also dramatic performances for entertainment and instruction presented by the *Arioi* society [Plate v]; the members of this society enjoyed practically unlimited sexual freedom, did not marry and practised infanticide. Sexes mixed freely (except during certain activities mentioned above, and during the preparation and eating of food), privacy was unknown and sexual play was indulged in from early childhood. J. Forster wrote: 'there is hardly a country to be found, where the young unmarried females are allowed such a latitude as at O-Taheitee and its neighbourhood in admitting a variety of young males, and abandoning themselves to various embraces without derogating from their character' (Forster, 1778, 491), and Cook commented, 'Both sexes express the most indecent ideas in conversation without the least emotion and they delight in such conversation beyond any other. Chastity indeed is but little Valued especially among the middle people' (Beaglehole, 1955, 128). Marriages took place between members of the same social class, and although marriage limited women's sexual freedom, particularly among the nobility, where the descent of the offspring was a matter of great concern, there were still many opportunities for affairs, and men were free to take secondary wives and concubines. Marriages were not regarded as permanent and spouses were changed frequently.

In a hedonistically-orientated society where such high value was placed on physical attractiveness, fitness, and on sexual gratification, old age was a social

44 (*top left*) Implement with bone blade for tattooing. Society Islands. *l.* 14 cm. *2062.* *Not from Cook's voyages*

45 (*bottom left*) Wooden tattooing mallet. Society Islands. *l.* 39 cm. *TAH 118*

46 Carved handle of a fly-whisk from Rurutu, Austral Islands. Similarly decorated fly-whisks, belonging to persons of high rank, were used in the Society Islands. *h.* 5 cm (figure only). *TAH 27*

disadvantage. Old or handicapped people were ridiculed and treated with contempt, and it was only after death that an individual was again the object of the community's attention. Bodies were either buried or exposed on a bier in special houses. Mourning was theatrically demonstrative; women gashed their heads and breasts with shark-tooth instruments in a show of grief. Sometimes a very impressive and rather strange ceremony was performed in which the chief mourner, dressed in a magnificent costume [Plate VI] and accompanied by blackened attendants in loincloths carrying clubs and spears, made rounds of the neighbourhood and terrorised the people. Banks participated in one such ceremony. After they had dressed up and blackened their bodies with candlenut soot, 'To the fort [Venus] then we went to the surprize of our freinds and affright of the Indians who were there, for they every where fly before the *Heiva* [chief mourner] like sheep before a woolf'. They progressed terrifying the people, who 'dispers'd every way, running to the first shelter, hiding themselves under grass or whatever else would conceal them', and finally, 'we repaird home, the *Heiva* undressd and we went into the river and scrubbed one another till it was dark before the blacking would come off' (Beaglehole, 1963, I, 289).

[63]

H	K	F	Courses	Winds	Remarks on Wednesday 12th Apl 1769
1	2		SW¾W		Calm & Cloudy hot sultry Weather
2				NW	Light airs next to a Calm with small rain
3	1				
4					
5	1		~		King Georges Island Extending from N WbW to S W Dist: 15 Lt
6					from the nearest shore 6 or 7 Leagues
7					
8					
9			Calm		
10					
11					
12			NW	Varble	Lightning all round the Compass
1	1	2	NW	Varble	
2	1	4	WbNW	orb	
3	1	4			
4	1	5	NWbW		
5	1	6			
6	1	6			Extreams of the Island from SSW to WbN
7	1	9	WNW		
8	1	6			
9	broke		WBN	SE	Severals of the Natives of the Island came off to us in their Canoes and
10	2				brought with them Cocoa Nuts and a Fruit very much like a
11					large Apple but did not eat not half so well, for these we gave them
12					Beds &ca

Extreams of the Island from _____ South & WBN ¼ N Dist from the nearest Island 5 Leg: Lat Ob 17.38

Course	Dist: said	Lat in	Long in pr acct	Long made b. Yor	Long made b. Yor
			D: 06.5	D: tue	D: 06.5
West	8 Miles	17.38	148.58		

H	K	F	Course	Winds	Remarks &c on Thursday 13 Apl
1	2		Calm		
2	1	3	NEbE	Variable	Cloudy and squally with Showers of rain
3	2	6	WBN		
4	2	4			the N E Point of Port Royal Bay W½N & Clarke point
5	2	4	West	N	S: 29 E: Distance of Shore 2 or 3 Leagues
6	2	6		EbS	
7	2	6			
8	2				Sounded got ground at 40 fath: 2 Remarkable Peaks SbW
9		6			
10		6			Sounded 15 fathom Rocky ground with course brown sand
11	1	6	W½S		brown sand and broken shells
12	1		WBS	West	D: 12.18. & 2 the 2 Peaks S½W dist: off shore 3 Miles. observed
1		2	SbW	SE	the Tide to Set from the WNW
2	2	4			Brought too maintopsail to the Mast
3	2	4			

Made sail for the Bay, at 6 hoisted out the Pinnace and sent her a head
to lay on the Shoal that is at the entrance of the Bay— at 7 Anchord in
the Bay in 13 fathom with the Best bower— a great number of the Natives
in their Canoes came off to the Ship bringing with them a few Coco Nutts and
other fruits and those they sumd &c at a great Dolly upon hoisted out the
Boat and land with a party of men under arms & Mr Banks and the other
Gentlemen in Company— Unbent the Stays: and all the small sails

47 Cook's log, showing the entry where he recorded the first sight of Tahiti ('King George's Island') on 12 April 1769. *Add. MS* 27955 *f.43*

48 Vessels of the island of 'Otaha' [Tahaa], Society Islands, by Sydney Parkinson, 1769.
Add. MS 23921 f.17

The Society Islands, and Tahiti in particular, have a special significance in Cook's voyages. He returned there repeatedly to replenish his supplies and to rest his men. This partiality for Tahiti can be easily understood for it was here that Cook and his men came into contact with Polynesians for the first time [47], and the impact of this apparently free-and-easy culture on the Europeans after eight months at sea must have been considerable. There was abundance of food in the islands, if not in one district, then in another, and the people – with few exceptions – remained friendly and welcoming [48].

Of course, things were not idyllic all the time. There were unpleasant incidents, most of which stemmed from the Tahitians' irrepressible predilection for thieving. Although stealing was a heavily-punishable offence in their society, at the same time a smart, audacious and skilfully carried out theft evoked admiration, and when Europeans were the victims it seems to have been treated almost as a sport. Only a day after anchoring at Matavai Bay Cook wrote 'Natives Flock'd about us in great Numbers and in as friendly a Manner as we could wish, only that they shew'd a great inclination to pick our pockets', and also 'in this they are prodiges expert' (Beaglehole, 1955, 78, 77). On the following day the first serious incident took place: the midshipman left in charge of the tent gave the order to fire when one of the

[65]

Tahitians snatched a musket, and the man was killed. 'When Mr Banks heard of the affair, he was highly displeased, saying, "If we quarrelled with those Indians, we should not agree with angels"; and he did all he could to accomodate the difference' (Parkinson, 1773, 15). Similar incidents, with varying degrees of seriousness, were to recur many times during Cook's voyages and one in Hawaii was finally to be the cause of his death. In Tahiti however when things went wrong the problem could usually be solved with the aid of friendly chiefs and priests, or by taking hostages, and after a while the balance would be restored and the Tahitians would return, smiling and friendly, eager to trade again.

Cook was remarkably open-minded, tolerant and fair in his dealings with the local people. In this he had strong support from his officers and 'the scientific gentlemen', who considered any such confrontations regrettable and abhorred bloodshed. The rule laid down for his crew in dealing with the inhabitants was 'To endeavour by every fair means to cultivate a friendship with the Natives and to treat them with all imaginable humanity' (Beaglehole, 1955, 75). At the same time he was firm, insisted on the stolen property being returned and did not tolerate insolence. He treated his own crew similarly: a man who broke into a store room and stole a large quantity of nails (which with hatchets, cloths and later, red feathers acquired in Tonga, were used in payment for food supplies) was given two dozen lashes; the butcher who threatened a woman with a reaping hook was punished too, in spite of the intervention of the injured party (the Tahitians could not bear to watch such physical punishment).

Leaving such clashes aside, life in the islands was pleasant for the seamen. They had to work hard but when they were free, they enjoyed themselves to the full. There was plenty of food, drink, entertainment and, of course, women. Their sexual generosity (which was not entirely disinterested, since the men had to reciprocate with gifts, and the rate increased as time went by), their men's connivance and indeed the whole sexual ethos of the place were probably the greatest source of wonder for the Europeans. During the first visit two seamen lost their heads to such an extent that they deserted for the sake of their sweethearts, but they were caught and given two dozen lashes each. When another man tried to abscond on the second voyage, Cook was more sympathetic; the man was without a family or friends, a drifter – 'where than can Such a Man spend his days better than at one of these isles where he can injoy all the necessaries and some of the luxuries of life in ease and Plenty' (Beaglehole, 1961, 404); he was put in irons for one night. A similar incident on the last voyage nearly had disastrous consequences for Cook himself, for when he followed his usual practice and took hostages – the local chief's pretty daughter, son and son-in-law – the people planned to seize him and Clerke at their daily bath. However the plan was given away by a local girl and failed.

Cook was realistic about the contacts between his men and the local women, and girls were tolerated; some of them even spent nights on the ship. He himself however stood aloof, and one of his men wrote: 'It has always been suppos'd that Cook himself, never had any connection with any of our fair friends; I have often seen them jeer and laugh at him, calling him Old, and good for nothing' (*ibid.*, 444, f.2). He was not easily shocked and he describes various scenes he witnessed with detached objectivity. He was, however, as were all the Europeans, shocked by customs of the *Arioi*, and describing them, he wrote, 'I must confess I do not expect to be believed as it is founded upon a Custom so inhuman and contrary to the first principals of human nature: it is this, that more than one half of the better sort of the inhabitants have enter'd into a resolution of injoying free liberty in love without being troubled or disturbed by its consequences . . . and the Children who are so unfortunate as to be thus begot are smother'd at the moment of their birth' (Beaglehole, 1955, 128). He, like the others, failed to understand the religious significance of the *Arioi*; but he was honest, for writing about religion he said that it 'is a thing I have learnt so little of that I hardly dare touch upon it' (*ibid.*, 134).

There was one aspect of fraternisation though which he treated very seriously and which was tragic in its consequences: venereal disease. Who was responsible for introducing this complaint to the islands – Wallis, Bougainville or Cook – has been the subject of much discussion, and the answer remains a moot point. That the three commanders (Cook in particular) tried to do everything they could to prevent it, is beyond doubt, but considering the prevalence of the disease in Europe at that time, the state of medical knowledge, the social background of ordinary seamen and the fact that infection rendered them liable to loss of pay, it would have been a miracle for a crew of any ship to be completely free of it. Moreover, it is now known that body fluids remain infectious from two to four years, and there are doubts about the extent to which spontaneous cure occurred or whether mercury compounds, applied then as a standard remedy, were effective, so that it is useless to apportion blame. Once Europeans found their way to the islands, contamination of the local population was inevitable.

In another respect too the Society Islands are somewhat different from the other islands visited by Cook. Here we meet more frequently Polynesians who are not just faceless chiefs or priests, or strange-sounding names, but real people, with personalities of their own. We encounter Purea (or Obarea), the favourite chiefess of Wallis, who also became a good friend to Cook and his men, and chief Tu, eventually the founder of the Tahitian royal dynasty as Pomare I; he asked Webber to paint a portrait of Cook, which he treasured for years. But the most interesting personality on the first voyage was Tupaia, a Raiatean noble and priest, who served as Cook's interpreter in the Pacific. It had been Banks' idea to take him

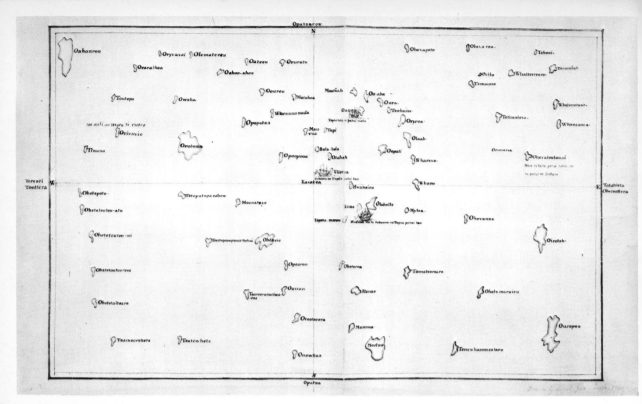

49 Map of the Society Islands and other archipelagos drawn, probably, by Cook and based on information given by the Raiatean, Tupaia, 1769. The islands are arranged schematically to indicate sailing time from Tahiti (in the centre). Remarks in Polynesian are noted by some islands. *Add. MS 21593 C*

on board, and he wrote, probably tongue in cheek: 'I do not know why I may not keep him as a curiosity, as well as some of my neighbours do lions and tygers at a larger expence than he will probably ever put me to; the amusement I shall have in his future conversation and the benefit he will be of to this ship . . . will I think fully repay me' (Beaglehole, 1963, 1, 312–13). Cook treated him more seriously: 'we found him to be a very intelligent person and to know more of the Geography of the Islands situated in these seas [49], their produce and the religion laws and customs of the inhabitants then any one we had met with . . . for these reasons and at the request of Mr Banks I received him on board together with a you[n]g boy his servant' (Beaglehole, 1955, 117). Tupaia was indeed of great help, as an interpreter both of the language and the culture, during the ship's visit to New Zealand. But Tupaia 'was, however, by no means beloved by the *Endeavour*'s crew, being looked upon as proud and austere, extorting homage, which the sailors, who thought themselves degraded by bending to an Indian, were very unwilling to pay, and preferring complaints against them on the most trivial occasions. On the contrary, his boy Tayota, was the darling of the ship's company from the highest to the lowest, being of a mild and docile disposition, ready to do any kind office for the meanest in the ship, and never complaining, but always pleased' (Marra, 1775, 219–20). Tupaia and Tayeto never reached England, they both died in Batavia.

50 Sir Joseph Banks (centre) with Omai and Dr Daniel Solander (right), by William Parry,
*c.*1775–6. *From the collection at Parham Park, West Sussex. Reproduced by kind permission.*

During the second voyage Cook again had an interpreter on board, a young man
from Borabora, called Odiddy or Hiti-Hiti, 'a youth of good parts . . . of a Docile,
Gentle and humane disposition, but in a manner wholy ignorant of their Religion,
Goverment, Manners, Customs and Traditions' (Beaglehole, 1961, 428). Odiddy,
who could not bring himself to leave the islands to go to England, was returned to
Raiatea before the voyage home and it was Omai, another young Raiatean, Captain
Furneaux's protegé on the *Adventure*, who became famous as the first Polynesian to
visit England. Furneaux handed him over to Banks on arrival, and soon after Omai
was launched into English society – he was introduced to the King, was entertained
by the best people and painted by Reynolds [**116**], was a house guest of the Earl of

Sandwich, went grouse-shooting, and was even set up in his own lodgings in London. He endeared himself to everybody, was very popular and amazed the English with his natural good manners and great sensitivity of feelings (whether real or assumed is another matter), in fact he was everything everybody expected and wanted him to be – the Noble Savage [50]. Omai was pleasant and likeable, but not particularly intelligent; he was of low rank and consequently not well-informed about his own society. It was probably just for these reasons that he found adjustment fairly easy, for it would be difficult to imagine the proud and dignified Tupaia kissing ladies' hands in London salons (British Museum, 1979, 81 ff.). Omai left England loaded with presents which included a suit of armour and some horses; his homecoming, however, was not happy. He used his newly-acquired wealth foolishly, giving presents to and associating with flatterers and people of low social standing, and ignoring or offending the influential chiefs who might have helped him. Cook and his men felt responsible for him and were very concerned about his future, so that when he finally decided to settle on Huahine, Cook had a European-style house built for him and a garden planted. However, he was never to amount to much in Tahitian society, and he died of natural causes about thirty months after Cook's departure.

Cook left the Society Islands with sad and tearful farewells. The evidence shows that on his last voyage his sense of fairness in dealing with the local people occasionally failed him, that he lost his temper much more quickly and more often, and that his reaction to the continual pilfering was sometimes out of all proportion to the crime committed (in retaliation for the theft of a goat he had some houses and war canoes burned and he ordered one particularly persistent thief to be punished by having his ears chopped off); but he was liked and respected by the islanders to the end. It is perhaps best to quote from his own journals again. When he was leaving the islands on his second voyage and thought that he would never come back, the people asked the name of his *marae*; 'I hesitated not one moment to tell him Stepney the Parish in which I lived when in London. I was made to repeated it several times over till they could well pronounce it, then Stepney Marai no Tootee was echoed through a hundred mouths at once . . . What greater proof could we have of these people Esteeming and loving us as friends whom they wishd to remember, they had been repeatedly told we should see them no more, they then wanted to know the name of the place were our bodies were to return to dust' (Beaglehole, 1961, 425–6).

3 New Zealand

DOROTA CZARKOWSKA STARZECKA

NEW ZEALAND, like Tahiti, was visited on all three of Cook's voyages. It was a convenient base for his forays into the Antarctic, but it was very different from the tropical Society Islands. The climate ranges from the sub-tropical in the north to the temperate in the south and it is thus, although mild by European standards, much cooler than that of other Pacific islands. The land is hilly or mountainous (the high mountains have a snowfall in winter, and there are permanent glaciers and snow-fields), well-watered, and in Cook's time mostly forested, with some areas of grassland and scrub.

Cook and his men were the first Europeans to set foot in New Zealand (although it was discovered by Tasman in 1642, he only coasted along most of its western side and never ventured to land), but the original discoverers and settlers of the country were Polynesians, who arrived, probably from Tahiti, about AD 750–780; later settlers probably came from the Marquesas. According to the Maori tradition, however, their ancestors reached New Zealand in the Great Fleet of named canoes about 1350, bringing with them cultivated plants and the dog (but no pigs). By the time of Cook's arrival, the culture which he encountered was the result of centuries of ingenious adaptation of a people from the tropics to the requirements of their new, comparatively cold, environment.

The Great Fleet is extremely important because the social organisation of the Maori largely derived from it. The whole population, which Cook estimated at 100,000, but which was probably more like 200,000–250,000, was divided into tribes, *iwi*. All the members of a tribe claimed descent from a common ancestor – the founder of the tribe and a member of the crew of one of the canoes in the Great Fleet. Tribes descended from those ancestors who reached New Zealand in the same canoe formed a kind of loose confederation called *waka* (canoe) and recognised certain obligations to help each other in emergencies though they often fought each other as well. The tribe was divided into subsections called *hapu*, again on the basis of descent from a common ancestor. The basic social unit was the household, usually consisting of a large family group called *whanau* with the oldest man, *kaumatua*, at its head. As in Tahiti, the social status of an individual depended on seniority of descent, traced preferably through the male line, so that those descended from the senior branches constituted an aristocracy – *rangatira* – the remainder being commoners – *tutua* or *ware*. There were also slaves – *taurekareka* – usually war captives without rights and treated as property. The tribe was ruled by chiefs with the help of high priests and the heads of households. Each *hapu* had one chief, also called *rangatira* (because he was the *rangatira* of his *hapu*); the most senior of them was called *ariki* and was the head of the tribe as a whole. The Maori chiefs, although not of direct divine descent like those in the Society Islands, were similarly surrounded with *tapu*, which was an equally important concept here. The other very important one was *mana* – spiritual or psychic power connected with rank, and some individual qualities, such as excellence in some field of activity. The fear of loosing *mana* and the desire to acquire more of it was a strong motivating agent. The *ariki* chiefs possessed *mana* in the highest degree, largely because of their rank. They could also acquire *mana* by successful administration of tribal affairs and thus increase the communal *mana* of the tribe.

The religious beliefs of the Maori were also a little different from those of the Society Islands. According to them, the earth (Papa – the female) and the sky (Rangi – the male) evolved out of the initial void. The gods, born from the union of Papa and Rangi, pushed the primeval parents apart, then quarrelled among themselves and during this quarrel their various activities created the world as it is now. The main gods were the same, with modifications, as in the Society Islands: Tane, the god of forests, the creator of mankind was the most important, Tu was the god of war; Rongo, the god of peace and agriculture; Tangaroa was the god of the sea, and there were others of lesser importance. These gods were shared by all the tribes, but each tribe also had its own tribal gods, and each family its own inferior, family gods which included deified ancestors and evil spirits. The gods could manifest themselves in natural phenomena or objects, as in the Society Islands, but manufactured images of gods were relatively rare, being made of stone or carved in wood in the form of a short peg terminating in an anthropomorphic head, and painted with red ochre; some of them had ornamental bindings and for worship they were adorned with red feathers. Priests were ranked according to the importance of the god whom they served.

Although religion was very important among the Maori, it never reached the heights of complexity and elaboration of the Tahitian rituals, and it was quite different in its material manifestations. The Maori sacred places, called *tuahu* (a variant of the Tahitian *ahu*, see p.52), usually took the form either of a heap of rough stones or of a post, sometimes surrounded with a fence, located in a secluded spot

CAPTAIN COOK
BY WEBBER

1 Captain James Cook by John Webber, artist on the third voyage.
*Reproduced by courtesy of the Warden and Brethren of the Hull
Trinity House. Photographed by Herbert Ballard.*

II *Resolution* and *Discovery* in Christmas Harbour, Kerguelen Island, by John Webber, 1776. *Add. MS 15513 f.3*

III View on the island of 'Eimeo' (Moorea), Society Islands, by John Webber, 1777. *Add. MS 15513 f.20*

IV Breast gorget, comprising a basketry base with feathers, shark-teeth and dog hair. Society Islands. *h.* 61 cm. *TAH 57*

V Two girls dancing in Tahiti, by John Webber, 1777. The drums are similar to that illustrated in 39. *Add. MS 15513 f.19*

VI Dress of the chief mourner, made of bark-cloth, with a feathered drape at the back and feather tassels at each side. The face-mask is of pearl-shell pieces; similar pieces decorate the crescent-shaped wood breast ornament from which is suspended a chest apron of pearl-shell slivers. The waist apron has decoration of polished coconut-shell pieces. The dress was presented to Cook during his second voyage and was given by him to the British Museum. Society Islands. *h.* 214 cm. *TAH 78*

VII Wood treasure box. New Zealand. *l.* 66 cm. *NZ 109*

VIII Wood canoe bailer. New Zealand. *l.* 50 cm. *NZ 123*

IX Bird-mask of wood, partially painted black and white, carved with a
human face on the underside of the lower jaw. Nootka Sound. *l.* 37 cm.
NWC 55

x Wood bowl carved with two handles in the form of people. The parallel
knifework on the bowl indicates that this belonged to a chief. Nootka
Sound. *l.* 20 cm. *1971 Am.5.1*

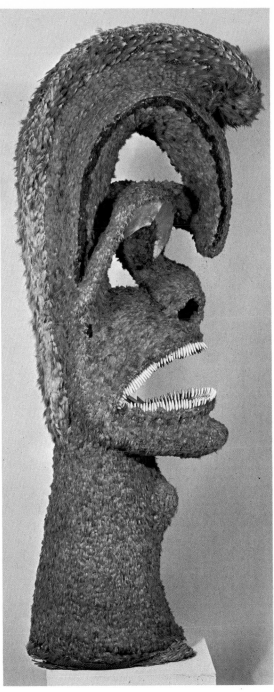

XI Feather image of a god. Hawaiian Islands.
h. 100·5 cm. *VAN 231*

XII Feather image of a god. Hawaiian Islands.
h. 107 cm. *LMS 221*

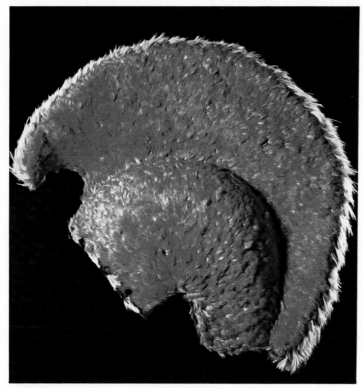

XIII Feather helmet. Hawaiian Islands. *l.* 38 cm. *HAW 108*

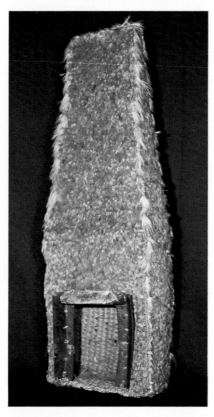

XIV Feather temple. This is the only object of its kind extant. Its use is not known, but it was undoubtedly connected with religious ceremonies. Hawaiian Islands. *h.* 59 cm. *Museum für Völkerkunde, Vienna. Cook–Sammlung no. 203. Photograph by Dr J. C. Wright, Bishop Museum, Honolulu.*

51 The inside of a *pa*, or fortified village, New Zealand, by John Webber, 1777.
Add. MS 15513 f.6

outside the village. The usual offering for the gods was vegetable food, sometimes dogs; important occasions demanded human sacrifice, although not as frequently as in the Society Islands; the victims were taken from among the slaves.

Maori settlements were also different. People lived in fortified villages called *pa* [51], situated defensively on hills or headlands, and protected by ramparts, stockades and ditches. Cook, describing one of them, comments, 'the Situation is such that the best Engineer in Europe could not have choose'd a better for a small number of men to defend themselves against a greater, it is strong by nature and made more so by Art' (Beaglehole, 1955, 197). Inside the *pa* houses were built around the central open space called *marae* (not to be confused with the Tahitian *marae*), which was used as a gathering place for community ceremonies and for receiving visitors. Each household consisted of a few separate houses which were simple and, as Cook recorded, 'better calculated for a cold than a hot climate: they are built low and in the form of an oblong square, the framing is of wood or small sticks and the sides and covering of thatch made of long grass. The door is generaly at one end and no biger than to admit a man to creep in and out; just within the door is the fire place and over the door or on one side is a small hole to let out the smook' (*ibid.*, 284).

[73]

Villages were fortified because of the more or less continual wars waged between the tribes. The causes were similar to those in the Society Islands, but the Maori were much quicker to take offence, and wars were very frequently fought to avenge insults and to obtain compensation. There were no professional warriors because every able-bodied man was trained from childhood in martial skills. Pitched battles were rarely fought, the preferred tactics being quick raids, ambuscades, and treachery. The success of a war was measured by the rank of the enemy killed, not by numbers. Weapons were designed primarily for hand-to-hand combat, and consisted mainly of clubs: long ones, made of wood, with a blade for striking and a point for stabbing, and short one-handed clubs of wood, bone or stone, with a spatulate blade and a carved grip [52–54]. Spears were also used, and whip-slings [55, 56] threw flaming darts into the besieged village to set fire to the houses. After the battle, the slain of the opposing tribe were eaten. This was almost the ultimate humiliation of the enemy because thus he lost his *mana* and was reduced to common food, but it was a greater disgrace still to be captured and become a slave. Heads of chiefs were preserved; those of enemies to be insulted and reviled, those of kinsmen to be wept over.

52 (*far left*) Wood club. New Zealand. *l.* 39 cm. NZ *91*

53 (*far centre*) Whalebone club. New Zealand. *l.* 32.5 cm. *St.827*

54 (*far right*) Basalt club. New Zealand. *l.* 40 cm. NZ *80*

55, 56 Wood whip-sling (and detail), used for throwing darts. The butt of the spear was lightly pushed into the ground and the spear inclined in the direction of flight. A short cord attached to the staff and terminating in a knot was passed round the spear-shaft so that the knot, held under the cord, gripped it. The thrower stood in front and hurled the spear with a sharp jerk over his shoulder. New Zealand. *l.* 149.5 cm. NZ *75*

The most highly valued vegetable food was *kumara* – sweet potato. Taro and yams were also cultivated but on a much smaller scale. The most important however was fern root – the rhizome of the bracken fern, a native plant which was the staple in the south where the sweet potato could not be grown, and a stand-by in the north when the sweet potato crop was exhausted. Fish was a very important part of the diet while other protein food was provided by birds, caught in various ingenious ways mostly incorporating nooses, rats which were caught in traps, dogs and human flesh. Cooking was done in earth ovens as in Tahiti, and there was a similar division of labour between the sexes.

In physical appearance the Maori resembled the Tahitians, although they were leaner; according to Cook, they had 'in general very good features' (*ibid.*, 278). Their clothes, however, were very different. Because the climate restricted the cultivation of the paper mulberry, barkcloth was scarce and used only for various minor objects like ear ornaments and kites (Tahitian barkcloth, brought by Cook's men, was in

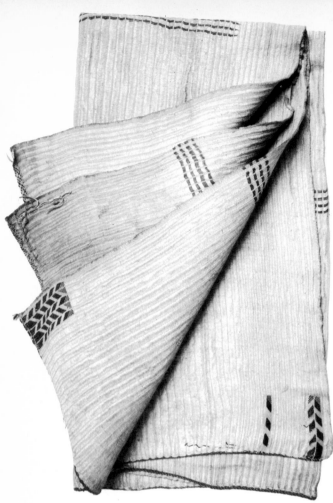

57 Flax cloak. New Zealand.
159 × 135 cm. *NZ 135*

58 A Maori with tattooed face, by
Sydney Parkinson, 1770.
Add. MS 23920 f.55

great demand in trading). Its place as a clothing material was taken by the native
'flax' (*Phormium tenax*), which was made into cloaks [57], kilts and belts by a plaiting
technique called finger-weaving (there were no looms). The usual Maori dress
consisted of two rectangular pieces, one wrapped round the waist and reaching
below the knee or to the heels, and the other worn over the shoulders as a cloak.
Some cloaks were very finely plaited and 'as stout as the strongest sail cloth' says
Cook (*ibid.*, 279); special ones were decorated with tags of cord, dog skin, feathers,
or with very fine coloured borders called *taniko*. Like the Tahitians, the Maori
decorated their bodies with tattoo (*moko*), but it was much more elaborate, especially
men's facial tattoo [58]. The main lines of the design had a carved effect, because in
tattooing the Maori used a different implement – the bone blade was shaped like a
miniature adze, and the design was incised, not punctured. Captain Cook was quite
appreciative; 'The figures they mostly use are spirals drawn and connected together
with great nicety and judgement; they are so exact in the application of these figures
that no difference can be found between the one side of the face and the other . . . The
women inlay the colour of black under the skins of their lips and both sexes paint

[76]

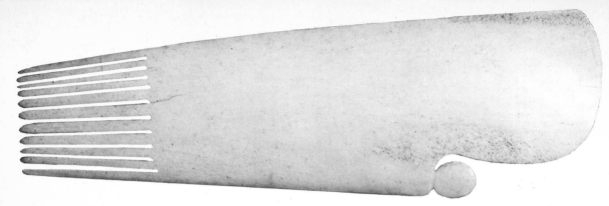

their faces and bodies at times more or less with red oker mix'd with fish oyle' (*ibid.*, 279). Banks had his own reasons for disapproving of this last custom among the women, it was 'universaly condemnd by us, for if any of us had unthinkingly ravishd a kiss from one of these fair Savages our transgressions were wrote in most legible Characters on our noses, which our companions could not fail to see on our first interview' (Beaglehole, 1963, II, 14). The men wore feathers or combs in their hair [59] and their most valued ornament was a neck pendant made of a whale tooth [61]. The most precious material was nephrite and various ornaments were made from it – neck pendants in the form of a stylised human figure [62], ear ornaments [60] and cloak pins. Such ornaments were family heirlooms and as they were handed down from generation to generation, they acquired more *mana* with each successive owner.

59 (*top*) Whalebone comb. New Zealand. *l.* 33 cm. *NZ 163*

60 (*above*) Nephrite ear ornament with two human teeth. New Zealand. *l.* 9 cm. *NZ 162*

61 (*below*) Whale-tooth neck pendant with vegetable-fibre cord and bone toggle. New Zealand. *l.* 14.5 cm. *NZ 159*

62 (*opposite*) Nephrite neck ornament with haliotis shell eyes, vegetable fibre cord and bone toggle. Given by Captain Cook to King George III. New Zealand. *l.* 7 cm. *From the collection of Her Majesty the Queen. Photograph: Commonwealth Institute*

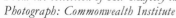

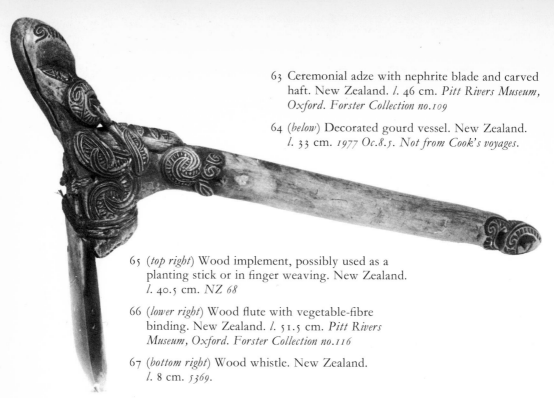

63 Ceremonial adze with nephrite blade and carved haft. New Zealand. *l.* 46 cm. *Pitt Rivers Museum, Oxford. Forster Collection no.109*

64 (*below*) Decorated gourd vessel. New Zealand. *l.* 33 cm. *1977 Oc.8.5. Not from Cook's voyages.*

65 (*top right*) Wood implement, possibly used as a planting stick or in finger weaving. New Zealand. *l.* 40.5 cm. *NZ 68*

66 (*lower right*) Wood flute with vegetable-fibre binding. New Zealand. *l.* 51.5 cm. *Pitt Rivers Museum, Oxford. Forster Collection no.116*

67 (*bottom right*) Wood whistle. New Zealand. *l.* 8 cm. *5369.*

Like the Tahitians, the Maori had no metal tools before the arrival of the Europeans, and yet there is a surprising difference in the extent and quality of their respective material cultures. Whereas in the Society Islands the creative genius of the people seems to have gone into elaboration of the social aspect of living – ceremonial and entertainment – and with a few exceptions relatively little care was given to objects, among the Maori this creativity found its expression in decorative arts, and above all in wood-carving. The Maori, like all the Polynesians, were sociable and gregarious people, and their social life, in general outline, was similar to that of the Tahitians, but not as complex. Instead, the Maori seemed to delight in decorating

nearly every object they used, and those which were left unadorned, some of the clubs for example, usually show purity of form and beautiful finish. This was noted in the journals of the Europeans. Parkinson expressed it very well: 'The men have a particular taste for carving: their boats, paddles, boards to put on their houses, tops of walking sticks, and even their boats valens, are carved in a variety of flourishes, turnings and windings, that are unbroken; but their favourite figure seems to be a volute, or spiral, which they vary many ways, single, double, and triple, and with as much truth as if done from mathematical draughts: yet the only instruments we have seen are a chizzel, and an axe made of stone. Their fancy, indeed, is very wild and extravagant, and I have seen no imitations of nature in any of their performances unless the head, and the heart-shaped tongue hanging out of the mouth of it, may be called natural' (Parkinson, 1773, 98). The tools used were indeed adzes with stone blades, stone and bone chisels, drills and gouges. The very carefully finished adzes, with carved hafts and highly polished nephrite blades [63], were never used as tools but were symbols of chiefly authority. The most common motifs in the carving were the human figure (which did not represent gods, but ancestors) and various curvilinear designs, with frequent use of spirals. Ornamental carving can be seen in domestic utensils – wooden bowls and gourd containers [64], implements [65] and weapons. Particular care was given to decoration of rectangular or oval wood treasure boxes with lids [Plate VII] in which personal ornaments were kept. Musical instruments, the most typical of which were wood flutes and whistles (there were no drums of the Tahitian type), were also nearly always decorated [66, 67]. The most magnificent carvings, however, were on canoes. The Maori canoe was a single-hull

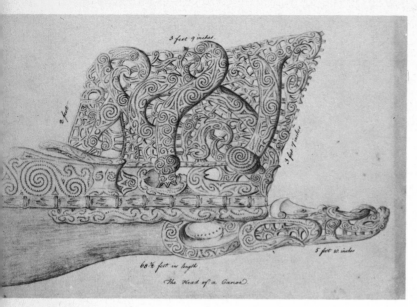

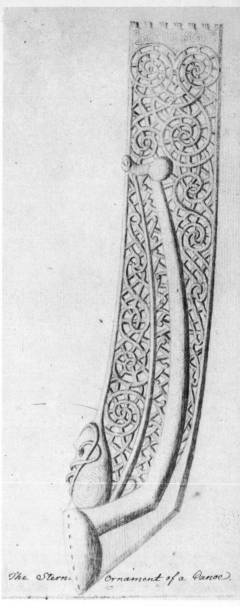

68 (*above*) Canoe prow ornament drawn by Hermann
Spöring, secretary to Joseph Banks on the first
voyage, 1770. *Add. MS 23920 f.77*

69 (*right*) A canoe stern ornament drawn by Spöring,
1770. *Add. MS 23920 f.78*

70 (*below*) Wood canoe paddle, decorated with
painting and carving. New Zealand. *l.* 179 cm.
NZ *150*

71 (*opposite*) New Zealand war canoe by Sydney
Parkinson, 1769–70. The bow and stern
ornaments are clearly shown (see 68, 69).
Add. MS 23920 f.46

dugout vessel made from a single tree trunk with added side planks. The smaller
ones, used for fishing, had a bow with carved human head and a plain upright stern
piece; the war canoes, much larger (the longest one Cook saw was 68.5 ft long), had
separate bow [68] and stern [69] sections, with a full human figure at the stem and
curvilinear, openwork designs on the high stern. Gunwale strakes, paddles [70] and
bailers [Plate VIII] were also decorated. Parkinson the draughtsman had a good eye
for detail: 'Their canoes had from eighteen to twenty-two men in them, and were
adorned with fine heads made out of a thick board, cut through like filligree-work,
in spirals of very curious workmanship [71]. At the end of this was a head, with two
large eyes of mother-of-pearl [it was haliotis], and a large heart-shaped tongue. This
figure went round the bottom of the board, and had feet and hands carved upon it
very neatly, and painted red: they had also high-peaked sterns, wraught in filligree,
and adorned with feathers, from the top of which depended two long streamers,
made of feathers, which almost reached the water' (*ibid.*, 93). Chiefs' houses were
also extensively decorated with carvings, and later, when the introduction of metal
tools eased the carvers' work, the carved meeting house, with painted rafters and
lattice wall panels, was to become the highest achievement of Maori carving.

The first meeting of the Europeans with the Maori was not very auspicious: Cook and his men landed in two boats and went over to some huts in the distance, and while they were gone a few native men appeared from the woods, frightening the seamen left in charge of the boats, who fired and killed one man. The next day, although contact was established, largely thanks to Tupaia who 'spoke to them in his own language and it was an [a]greeable surprise to us to find that they perfectly understood him' (Beaglehole, 1955, 169), the local people remained belligerent and insolent, and when some shots were fired again, a few people were wounded and the Maori disappeared. Cook then decided to go out in a boat a little farther 'if possible to surprise some of the natives and to take them on board and by good treatment and presents endeavour to gain their friendship' (*ibid.*, 170). Two canoes were sighted and Cook ordered 'a Musquet to be fire'd over their heads thinking that this would either make them surrender or jump over board, but here I was misstaken for they immidiatly took to thier arms' (*ibid.*, 170). As the result, 'two or three' of the Maori were killed, and the three who jumped overboard, were taken to the ship to be clothed and fed, to which they responded very cheerfully. Banks, having described the incident, finished: 'Thus ended the most disagreable day My life has yet seen, black be the mark for it and heaven send that such may never return to embitter future reflection' (Beaglehole, 1963, I, 403). Cook, obviously grieved, tried to justify his actions: 'I am aware that most humane men who have not experienced things of this nature will cencure my conduct in fireing upon the people in this boat nor do I my self think that the reason I had for seizing upon her will att all justify me, and had I thought that they would have made the least resistance I would not have come near them, but as they did I was not to stand still and suffer either my self or those that were with me to be knocked on the head' (Beaglehole, 1955, 171). The difficulty was that in the Maori Cook met men for whom fighting was a way of life, an unavenged insult was unthinkable, and they were continually on their guard ready to react when an opportunity arose. Even though friendship was eventually established, this element of uncertainty between the Maori and the Europeans persisted, and is reflected in the comments made about the Maori. Banks was impressed by their 'open countenance' and their friendliness, and, when two Maori decided to spend the night on the ship, he writes 'I was prejudicd much in their favour and surely such confidence could not be found in the breasts of designing people' (Beaglehole, 1963, I, 414), but a few days later he writes that they are 'most abominably saucy, continualy threatening us' (*ibid.*, I, 439). Cook writes that they 'would not enter into a friendly traffick with us, but would cheat when ever they had an opertunity' (Beaglehole, 1955, 212), but later 'All this fore noon had abundance of the Natives about the Ship and some few on board, we trafficked with them for a few trifles in which they dealt very fair and friendly' (*ibid.*, 216). However the Maori were realistic and quick to learn and a *modus vivendi* was usually established after Cook had made an initial show of strength. As Banks wrote, 'they Always after one nights consideration have acknowledgd our superiority but hardly before' (Beaglehole, 1963, I, 442), and were 'most perfectly civil . . . where we were known but never where we were not' (*ibid.*, 435). The Maori usually went through the same routine when meeting the Europeans for the first time. There was the standard welcome call: 'Haere mai ki uta kia patua' – 'Come ashore and be clubbed', and then the obligatory performance of frightening the enemy [72], which Anderson describes very well: 'Before they begin the onset they join in a war song to which they all keep the exactest time, and in a short space raise their passion to a degree of frantic fury attended with the most horrid distortion of their eyes, mouths and tongues to strike terror in their enemies, which to those who have not seen such a practice makes them appear more like infernal daemons than men and would almost chill the boldest with fear' (Beaglehole, 1967, 814). Tupaia was of enormous help to Cook in establishing friendly relations with the Maori. He interpreted, explained, smoothed things over, and must have impressed them considerably, particularly with his knowledge of Polynesian lore, for he was popular and respected. When Cook returned to New Zealand on his second voyage, they asked about Tupaia and were apparently saddened to hear of his death.

Here, as in the Society Islands, Cook was fair in dealing with people. When three sailors dug up some potatoes in the native gardens during their shore duty, they were punished with a dozen lashes each and 'the first of the three I remited back to confinement because he insisted that their was no harm in what he had done' (Beaglehole, 1955, 216). He saw plainly that contacts with the Europeans brought about changes in their culture, and that these changes were not for the better. During his second voyage he wrote about the Maori: 'During our short stay in this Sound I have observed that this Second Visit of ours hath not mended the morals of the Natives of either Sex, the Women of this Country I always looked upon to be more chaste than the generality of Indian Women, whatever favours a few of them might have granted to the crew of the Endeavour it was generally done in a private manner and without the men seeming to interest themselves in it, but now we find the men are the chief promoters of this Vice, and for a spike nail or any other thing they value will oblige their Wives and Daughters to prostitute themselves . . . we debauch their Morals already too prone to vice and we interduce among them wants and perhaps diseases which they never before knew and which serves only to disturb that happy tranquillity they and their fore Fathers had injoy'd. If any one denies the truth of this assertion let him tell me what the Natives of the whole extent of America have gained by the commerce they have had with Europeans' (Beaglehole, 1961, 174–5).

72 (*overleaf*) New Zealand war canoe 'bidding defiance to the ship', by Sydney Parkinson, 1769–70. *Add. MS 23920 f.50*

There was one Maori custom which held a grim fascination for the Europeans – cannibalism. Its existence was apparent during the first visit, and on the second voyage Cook and his men actually witnessed it. One day, during Cook's absence, 'the gentlemen' brought on board a human head – leftovers of a Maori feast – and here 'a peice of the flesh had been broiled and eat by one of the Natives in the presince of most of the officers'. When Cook returned to the ship, 'the sight of the head and the relation of the circumstances just mentioned struck me with horor and filled my mind with indignation against these Canibals, but when I considered that any resentment I could shew would avail but little and being desireous of being an eye wittness to a fact which many people had their doubts about, I concealed my indignation and ordered a piece of the flesh to be broiled and brought on the quarter deck where one of these Canibals eat it with a seeming good relish before the whole ships Company which had such effect on some of them as to cause them to vomit' (*ibid.*, 293).

Later the Europeans received more proof of this custom than they bargained for. During Furneaux's stay in Queen Charlotte Sound, where he narrowly missed Cook at their rendezvous, the whole crew of a cutter – ten men – were murdered and eaten. When Cook returned later, after the *Adventure* had already sailed, he was unaware of what had happened although he noticed a certain wariness on the part of the local people. When the *Resolution* returned to New Zealand on the third voyage, the knowledge of this unhappy incident made the sailors reluctant to pursue some of their usual amusements, rather to Cook's satisfaction: 'Their [the Maori's] articles of commerce were Curiosities, Fish and Women the two first always came to a good market, which the latter did not: the Seamen had taken a kind of dislike to these people and were either unwilling or affraid to associate with them; it had a good effect as I never knew a man quit his station to go to their habitations' (Beaglehole, 1967, 61). Cook, as always, tried to see the problem of cannibalism objectively, and if he could not excuse, then he tried to explain it as a survival of a savage custom from the past, emphasising at the same time the good points of the Maori. He decided not to carry out reprisals: 'I should think no more of it as it was some time sence and done when I was not there' (*ibid.*, 69).

4 The Nootka of Vancouver Island

J. C. H. KING

THE west coast of North America, New Albion, had first been optimistically claimed by Sir Francis Drake for the English Crown in the sixteenth century and it was a major purpose of Cook's third voyage to explore the rivers and inlets of that coast between latitudes 45° and 65° north to find a 'water passage' leading to Hudson's Bay or thereabouts. In pursuit of this, Cook was ordered to 'put into the first convenient Port to recruit your Wood and Water and procure Refreshments' (Beaglehole, 1967, ccxxi). So, on 29 March 1778, after a seven-week voyage from the Hawaiian Islands, he put into an 'inlet' having 'resolved to anchor to endeavour to get some Water, of which [we] were in great want' (*ibid.*, 295). This inlet is now known as Nootka Sound and it is situated at about 49° 40′ latitude on the west coast of Vancouver Island. It had probably been visited in 1774 by Juan Pérez in the *Santiago* on his way home from the Queen Charlotte Islands.

A base was established at Resolution Cove on Bligh Island on 31 March [73] and Cook set about his immediate concern, the repair of the ships, for which there was an abundant supply of timber (he had remarked in his journal that this 'sea Coast, high as well as low, was cloathed with wood' (*ibid.*, 294)). Rotten wood had to be removed and replaced, the foremast needed repairs while the mizzenmast had to be entirely renewed from a tree selected from those growing nearby. This work took nearly a month, so that there was plenty of time to take stock of their surroundings and the local population.

The abundant resources of timber and food on that coast are a product of the warm sea current and heavy rainfall, and they provided subsistence for what was one of the densest populations of any hunter-gatherer societies. The Nootka on the west coast of Vancouver Island belong, with the closely related Makah and the neighbouring Kwakiutl, to the Wakashan language group. However it seems likely that these two terms, recorded by Cook, were based on his misunderstanding of the words 'Nootka-a', meaning 'go round', which may have been uttered as advice to the Europeans searching for an anchorage, and 'Wak'ash', an expression of friendship.

[89]

73 (*overleaf*) The *Resolution* in Resolution Cove, Bligh Island, Nootka Sound, by John Webber, 1778. *Add. MS 15514 f.10*

74 The village of Yuquot in Nootka Sound, by John Webber, 1778. *Add. MS 15514 f.7*

Cook interpreted them as being the names of the place and the people. The people whom Cook encountered in Nootka Sound belonged to a group known as the Moachat confederacy. The northern Nootka are made up of a number of such confederacies each consisting of several villages; each village contained a number of families whose members all had a common name and a tradition of descent from a common ancestor. Inheritance was traced through the male line and political power was vested in the highest ranking chief. The lineages of a confederacy normally had a common winter village where feasting and dancing took place. In this respect, however, the Moachat confederacy was an exception to the rule at the time of Cook's visit. At that date the Moachat remained all year in small settlements along the coast like Yuquot, the Moachat village visited twice by Cook [**74**]. Cook did not have dealings with members of other confederacies, such as the Muchalat, whose territory lay further inland, as the Moachat were determined to keep the profitable trade with the Europeans for themselves.

The Nootka were dependent on fish for their food, especially salmon and herring, and the method used to catch the herring, which were in season at the time, was unusual enough to be described in some detail by the visitors who observed it. They used 'an instrument some thing like an Oar; it is 20 feet long, four or five Inches broad and about half an inch thick, each edge for about two thirds of its length, (the other third being the handle) is set with bone teeth about two inches long. This instrument they strike into a Shoal of small fish, who are caught either between or upon the teeth' (*ibid.*, 320). Halibut were caught on hooks of wood-roots, which were steamed and bent into a U-shape. Whales were hunted by Nootkan chiefs; although this was not a significant subsistence activity it was important for their status and was surrounded by ceremony. The visitors admired the whale harpoons, which had heads of mussel shell [75], and Clerke recorded details of the hunt: 'They told us the method they made use of to manage these enormous Animals; which was by means of a Harpoon (some of which they sold us) composed of bone and shell,

75 Whaling harpoon of mussel-shell, with bone barbs and a line of sinew, leather, nettle-fibre and cherry bark. Nootka Sound. *w*. 35 cm (when coiled). *NWC 76*

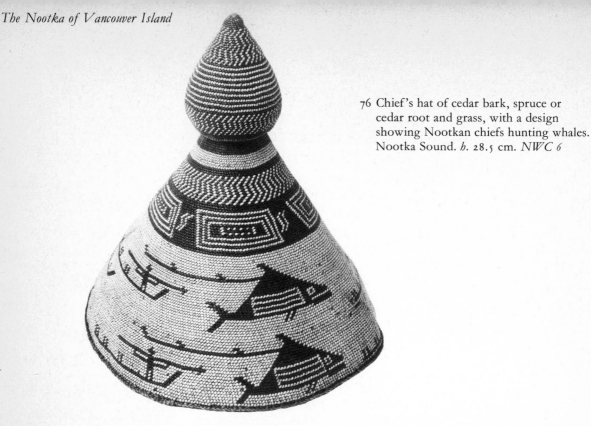

76 Chief's hat of cedar bark, spruce or cedar root and grass, with a design showing Nootkan chiefs hunting whales. Nootka Sound. *h.* 28.5 cm. *NWC 6*

made exceeding sharp, and indeed a compleat Instrument for the purpose; this is firmly fix'd to a strong Cord, at the other end of which is fast either a large Bladder, or something so compact as to answer the same purpose, by holding a quantity of Air, and by that means becoming very buoyant . . . into a Cavity of this Harpoon is stuck a strong Spear, with which it is forced into the Whale; the Spear disengaging itself, the Harpoon is left in him & they pursue & worry him by means of the bladder' (*ibid.*, 1324–25). Whale hunting, and other scenes, were depicted in the basketry of the hats worn by chiefs [**76**], and these drew from Cook a general comment on the rich culture he had encountered: 'We have sometimes seen the whole process of their whale-fishery painted on the caps they wear. This, though rudely executed, serves, at least, to shew, that though there be no appearance of the knowledge of letters amongst them, they have some notion of a method of commemorating and representing actions, in a lasting way, independently of what may be recorded in their songs and traditions' (Cook and King, 1784, II, 327).

As one might expect in such an environment, dug-out canoes were of great importance: large ones were used for trading, small ones for fishing, and others for hunting whales. War, too, was waged by canoe and was principally conducted by means of raids on other villages. The variety of their weapons for war excited general comment amongst the sailors [**77, 78**]: 'Their weapons are bows and arrows [**79**], slings, spears, short truncheons of bone, somewhat like the *patoo patoo* of New Zealand [**80**], and a small pick-axe, not unlike the common American *tomahawk*. The

77 (*above*) Ceremonial club of wood inlaid with teeth and human hair, carved with a wolf's head holding a human head in its jaw. (?) Nootka Sound. *l.* 53 cm. *NWC 100*

78 (*left*) Wood club (?) carved with a bird finial, perhaps used to kill fish after they were caught. Nootka Sound. *l.* 56 cm. *NWC 37*

79 (*right*) Arrow box. The lid is incised with a design of three intertwined people. Nootka Sound. *l.* 93 cm. *Museum für Völkerkunde, Vienna. Cook-Sammlung no.215*

80 (*far right*) Whalebone club, the most typical Nootkan fighting weapon. Nootka Sound. *l.* 51.5 cm. *NWC 42*

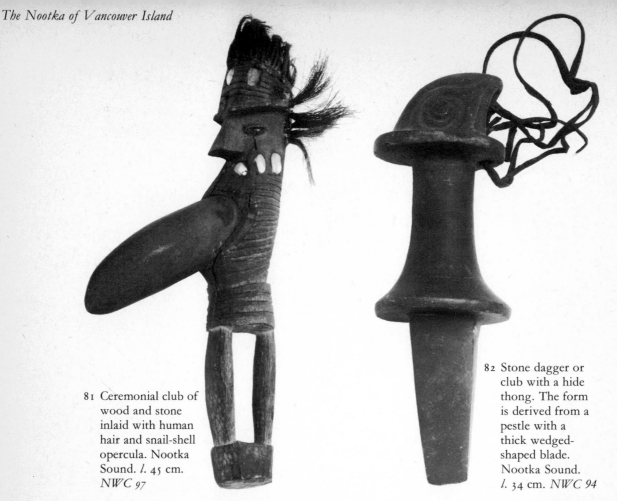

81 Ceremonial club of
wood and stone
inlaid with human
hair and snail-shell
opercula. Nootka
Sound. *l.* 45 cm.
NWC 97

82 Stone dagger or
club with a hide
thong. The form
is derived from a
pestle with a
thick wedged-
shaped blade.
Nootka Sound.
l. 34 cm. *NWC 94*

spear has generally a long point, made of bone . . . The tomahawk [81] is a stone, six
or eight inches long, pointed at one end, and the other end fixed into a handle of
wood. This handle resembles the head and neck of the human figure; and the stone is
fixed in the mouth, so as to represent an enormously large tongue. To make the
resemblance still stronger, human hair is also fixed to it. This weapon they call
taaweesh, or *tsustkeeah*. They have another stone weapon [82] called *seeaik*, nine inches
or a foot long, with a square point' (*ibid.*, 324).

The sea and its products played an important part in Nootka life since it provided
all the major food resources; no plants were domesticated. However, they depended
heavily on the land for other essential materials, particularly wood. Berries, such as
the salmon berry (*Rubus spectabilis*), were considered a delicacy and could be
preserved for considerable periods. Capes [83] and cloaks [84], the most common
forms of clothing for both sexes, were made by women from the shredded bark of
the yellow cedar interwoven with nettle fibre. Fur and skin from such land mammals
as the wolf, fox, martin, ermine and deer, wool from the mountain goat and the fur
of the sea otter were also used both for clothing and for the decoration of cedar bark
clothing.

83 Cape of yellow cedar bark. Nootka Sound. max. *w.* 75 cm. *NWC 50*

84 Cloak of yellow cedar bark, with geometric decoration of goat's wool and painted design representing (?) a raven and two flatfish. Nootka Sound. *w.* 152 cm. *NWC 53*

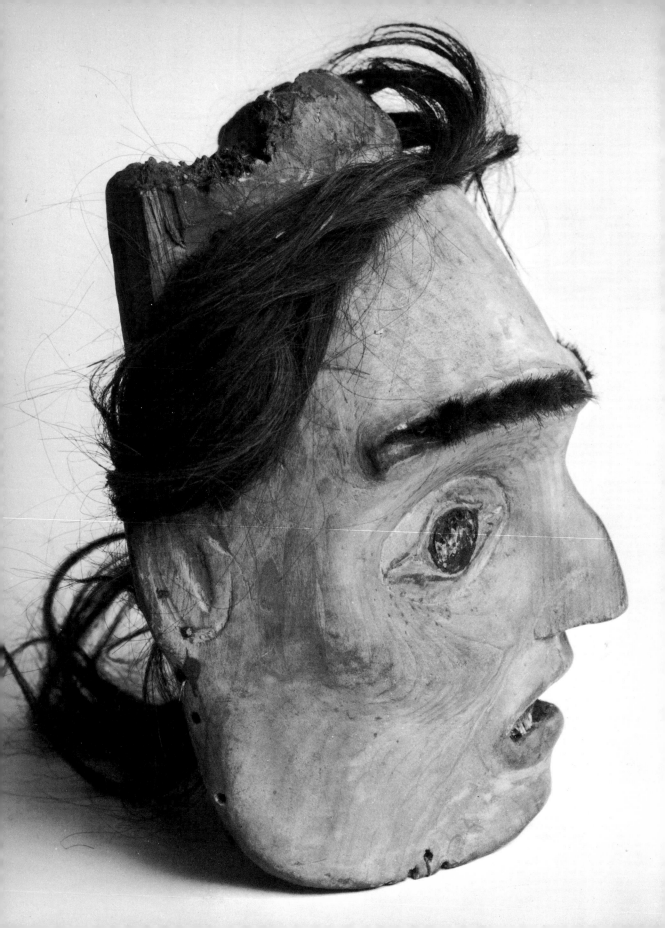

86 Interior of a house at Yuquot, Nootka Sound, by John Webber, 1778. *Peabody Museum of Archaeology and Ethnology, Harvard University. Photograph: Hillel Burger*

With such abundant supplies to hand, objects were naturally made of wood: red cedar, split into planks, was used to construct the large houses [86] which so impressed Cook and his fellow voyagers, while alder and other woods were used for elaborately carved food or oil bowls [Plate x], for ceremonial masks [Plate ix; **85**], rattles [**87**] and for large decorated storage boxes. These were made by scoring,

87 Bird-rattle of wood painted black, red and white. It was carved in two parts which were held together with hide ties. Nootka Sound. *l.* 47.5 cm. *NWC 28*

85 Human face-mask of wood, with human hair, mica decoration and teeth of split bird-quills. Nootka Sound. *h.* 24 cm. *NWC 57*

88 Wood storage box of Nootkan or Kwakiutl origin. This type of box was made by kerfing, or cutting, and bending a single piece of wood into shape. 58.5 × 61 × 46.5 cm. *61.3–12.41. Not from Cook's voyages*

steaming and bending a single plank to form the body of the box, the lid and the base being constructed separately [88]. Artefacts were acquired in large numbers by the crews of the two ships; most were utilitarian, such as fish hooks, combs [90] and a sun-visor [89], but others represented animals and mythological beings from the supernatural world. Initially the Nootka were furtive about selling such things, but their reluctance decreased in the face of European avidity. Samwell recorded the use of theatrical deceit to enhance the price of a bird mask: '. . . one of them today put up before his face an image of a bird's head & offered it for sale, at the same time shaking it up and down, while another person sitting by him applyed a small whistle to his Belly so as to collect the air by drawing the Skin round it & immitated in some measure the whistling of a bird; this being supposed to be done by some curious Contrivance raised the Value of it so much in the Eye of one of our collectors of Curiosities, that he immediately offered a very large price for it which was as quickly accepted of by the cunning Indian' (Beaglehole, 1967, 1091).

89 Sun-visor made of the quills of eagle feathers bound around the edge with hide. Nootka Sound. *w.* 28 cm. *NWC 12*

90 Wood comb carved on each side with a human face. Nootka Sound. *l.* 21 cm. *NWC 105*

Such objects were made with adzes and knives some of which had iron blades and this gave rise to considerable speculation as to how iron might have reached the area. The first possibility was that it had been acquired from the Spanish four years earlier, an idea which Cook was almost certainly right in dismissing because the Nootka were, he thought, too practised in the use of iron to have only had it for such a short time. Otherwise iron may have reached the Nootka by trade from the British and French settlements in the east, from the Spanish in California, or even from Russia, China or Japan in the west. Examination of two eighteenth-century knives has shown that they are made of layers of iron and steel cold-hammered, but has not revealed any further evidence of origin.

The Nootka showed a particular aptitude for trade; they began almost as soon as the ships entered the Sound and continued trading until they departed. Metal was their prime requirement, initially iron and then brass: 'Hardly a bit of it [brass] was left in the ships, except what belonged to our necessary instruments. Whole suits of clothes were stripped of every button; bureaus of their furniture; and copper kettles, tin cannisters, candlesticks, and the like, all went to wreck; so that our American friends here got a greater medley and variety of things from us, than any other nation whom we had visited' (Cook and King, 1784, II, 279). The Nootka showed not the slightest interest in the glass beads which had been brought for trading. Their aptitude for trade was abetted by a highly developed sense of property; when buying fodder for the animals Cook remarked humorously that 'there did not seem to be a single blade of grass, that had not a seperate owner' (*ibid.*, 284). In exchange, the Europeans obtained food, water and wood, as well as artefacts and pelts, but by the time they left, prices in terms of European commodities had risen considerably, such was the astuteness of the Nootka.

They observed relatively little of Nootkan life apart from trading activities and herring fishing and of what they saw the most important features were the ceremonies and ritual with which the chiefs and people of Yuquot greeted the European ships, both on arrival and each morning when they came out to visit and trade. On March 30 King noted that the songs and speeches of a man in one of the canoes indicated pleasure at the arrival of the Europeans: 'The first men that came woud not approach the Ship very near & seemd to eye us with Astonishment, till the second boat came that had two men in it; the figure & actions of one of these were truly frightful; he workd himself into the highest frenzy, uttering something between a howl & a song, holding a rattle in each hand, which at intervals he laid down, taking handfulls of red Ocre & birds feathers & strewing them in the Sea; this was follow'd by a Violent way of talking, seemingly with vast difficulty in uttering the Harshest, & rudest words, at the same time pointing to the Shore, yet we did not attribute this incantation to threatning or any ill intentions towards us; on the contrary they seem'd quite pleas'd with us' (Beaglehole, 1967, 1394). This ceremony was probably part of the ritual attached to the welcoming of a visiting chief on arrival for a feast or *potlatch*. Later visitors, particularly fur traders, observed the same ceremony, frequently becoming irritated at the length of time that had to pass in this way before trading could begin. A minor but interesting aspect of the welcome ceremonies was the interest by the British in the Indian music and vice versa. Although Cook, King and others refer to the harshness of some of the songs and speeches, Cook also talks of songs sung as a 'peaceable amusement' as having 'a very pleasing effect' (*ibid.*, 315). Conversely, the Indians appreciated European music. One evening King and others listened to 'A young man with a remarkable soft effeminate voice' who repeated his song several times because of the attention it received', (*ibid.*, 315). 'As they were now very attentive & quiet in list'ning to their diversions, we judg'd they might like our musick, & we orderd the Fife & drum to play a tune; these were the only people we had seen that ever paid the smallest attention to those or any of our musical Instruments . . . they Observd the Profoundest silence, & we were sorry that the Dark hind'red our seeing the effect of this musick on their countenances' (*ibid.*, 1394–95).

After a day or two of contact the Nootkans lost their fear of the strangers, and came on board and mixed freely. This gave the sailors opportunity to observe and remark on the physical characteristics of the Indians, particularly of their women. Clerke noted that: 'These are the dirtiest set of People I ever yet met with . . . A Girl, who was a Week or 10 days on board the Ship, with one of the Officers, was taken great pains with . . . after a score [of] good scrubings she was a very different Creature to what she appear'd when first taken in hand; her colour was then very near as white as our own . . . but they have clap'd on so compleat a mask of dirt as to render the ground work an impenetrable secret' (*ibid.*, 1326). Clerke was relatively restrained in his comments whereas Samwell allowed his lechery to break into the flow of his journal: 'we sometimes found some Jewels that rewarded our trouble, Namely two sparkling black Eyes accompanied with a beautiful Face, & when such was our fortune we never regretted the time & trouble it had cost us in digging through loads of red Oaker, Soot & other Dirt' (*ibid.*, 1100). The women referred to were probably slaves, that is people who were captured or acquired by trade, since in general the explorers commented on the modesty of the women.

More significant than the observations on the appearance of the Nootkans were the comments by Cook and others on the society, religion and language of the Indians. Cook, as always, regretted that he did not find out more: 'Of the Goverment and Riligion of these people, it cannot be supposed that we could learn much' he says (*ibid.*, 322), but he observes that there were chiefs to whom others were subordinate, and that this authority extended only to their family. Cook was

91 (*left*) Wood figure of woman and child. Nootka Sound. The significance of these figures (91–94) is not known. *h.* 27.5 cm. *NWC 64*

92 (*below*) Wood figure of woman and child. Nootka Sound. *h.* 16 cm. *NWC 63*

93 (*right*) Wood figure of woman and child. Nootka Sound. *h.* 38 cm. *NWC 66*

94 (*far right*) Wood figure of woman and child. Nootka Sound. *h.* 16 cm. *NWC 62*

correct in this brief mention of social organisation, as he was also about the hereditary nature of the office of Chief (which he deduced because of the youth of some of the chiefs).

Less was learnt about religion; on one of the visits to Yuquot the interior of a house was painted by Webber [85] and in the background of the picture are two house posts carved with human figures. The Nootka were very secretive about these, which gave rise to the speculation that they represented gods. Cook was not so sure: 'I am not altogether of that opinion, at least if they were they hild them very cheap, for with a small matter of iron or brass, I could have purchased all the gods in the place, for I did not see one that was not offered me, and two or three of the very smalest sort I got' (Beaglehole, 1967, 319–20). The purpose of these small figures [91–94] is unknown, but they were probably not of a religious importance. Northwest Coast religion is characterised by relatively vague beliefs about deities and cosmology, combined with very specific concern for the immortality of economically important species of land and sea animals. These beliefs involved the performance of rituals designed to ensure the annual return of the animals and fish. In them the chiefs took the central role. Shrines were set up containing images of animals over which chiefs might hold some power; and in these shrines chiefs would fast and pray, for example, for the return of the herring in spring. In his short stay at Yuquot Cook learnt nothing of this.

When the repairs to the ships were finished and enough food – for the sheep and goats as well as the crew – had been collected the ships set sail. The relations between the Indians and Europeans had remained good, apart from some relatively minor quarrels. Nobody had been killed, though King pointed out that 'we never before gave so great a latitude to insolent behaviour as we did to these' (*ibid.*, 1407). Probably the worst legacy provided by the British was not any venereal disease which may have been given to the female slaves, but the discovery of the place itself and its consequent importance in the fur trade. In describing his parting with one of the chiefs, Cook adumbrates what was to come: 'before he went I made him up a small present and in return he present[ed] me with a Beaver skin [sea otter skin] of greater value, this occasioned me to make some addition to my present, on which he gave me the Beaver skin Cloak he had on, that I knew he set a value upon. And as I was desireous he should be no suffer[er] by his friendship and generosity to me, I made him a present of a New Broad Sword with a brass hilt which made him as happy as a prince. He as also many others importuned us much to return to them again and by way of incouragement promised to lay in a good stock of skins for us' (*ibid.*, 307–8).

Further sea otter pelts were acquired in Prince William Sound in Alaska during the summer of 1778 [95], and the readiness with which these could be sold to the

[107]

5 Woman of Prince William Sound, by John Webber, 1778.
Add. MS 15514 f.11

Russians of Kamchatka and the Chinese in Canton, where King estimated that he sold skins to a value of £2000, enhanced the attractions of the source of supply. The publication of the events of the voyage after the return home led to numerous trading expeditions to the Northwest Coast in search of furs in the 1780s, but generally speaking the Nootka were left free of European interference until the colonisation of British Columbia in the nineteenth century.

5 Hawaii

DOROTA CZARKOWSKA STARZECKA

THE Hawaiian Islands were considered by Cook to be his most important
discovery. The archipelago consists of a chain of islands stretching from the
north-west to the south-east across the Tropic of Cancer in the eastern half of
the Pacific, and was sighted on 18 January 1778. The eight inhabited islands – the
most important of which are Hawaii, Maui, Kauai and Oahu – are mountainous, of
volcanic origin (there are two active volcanoes) with a sub-tropical climate
conditioned by the north-east tradewinds. The windward side of the island is
forested where not cultivated, while the dry leeward side is mostly grassland and
scrub.

The people inhabiting the islands were Polynesians, as Cook realised at once: 'At
this time we were in some doubt whether or no the land before [us] was inhabited,
this doubt was soon cleared up, by seeing some Canoes coming off from the shore
towards the Ships, I immediately brought to to give them time to come up, there
were three and four men in each and we were agreeably surprised to find them of the
same Nation as the people of Otahiete and the other islands we had lately visited'
(Beaglehole, 1967, 263–4).

The islands were already populated by AD 500, probably from the Marquesas,
with some later immigration from the Society Islands, and the culture of the
immigrants exhibited the common Polynesian traits: a stratified society, subsistence
based on agriculture and fishing, a religious system which radically influenced social
organisation. Thus Hawaiian society was divided into four classes: *ali'i* – chiefs and
nobles, considered to be of divine origin; *kahuna* – priests and master-craftsmen;
maka'ainana – commoners, cultivators and fishermen; and *kauwa* – slaves and
outcasts. Desire to achieve the highest possible rank was so strong among chiefs that
marriages were sometimes arranged between brother and sister if such a union could
produce offspring of more exalted social rank. The origins of the lowest class, the
outcasts, is not clear – possibly they were law-breakers or maybe war captives; like
the slaves in New Zealand, they were outside society, and their ranks supplied

sacrificial victims. Society was governed according to religious laws usually described as the *kapu* system (*kapu* is the Hawaiian form of *tapu*, and has the same meaning). The islands were divided into independent chiefdoms, at the head of which stood a supreme chief called *ali'i nui* or *moi*. He ruled through minor chiefs and their executives who were directly responsible for the efficient functioning of the economy. The bulk of the population, the commoners, had no voice in political matters.

In Hawaii we again meet the common Polynesian deities: Kane, creator of nature and men; associated with him was Tangaloa, a god of relatively little importance; Ku, god of war and a special god of the chiefs; and Lono, god of peace and agriculture. These cosmic deities were here known under the name *akua.*' *Aumakua* were family gods, often deified ancestors, and were worshipped by commoners in their household shrines. In practical terms the most important among the *akua* were Lono and Ku, for the open-air temples, here called *heiau*, were dedicated either to one or the other. It was only in the temples dedicated to Ku that human sacrifices were offered; for Lono, foodstuffs and barkcloth were sufficient. The Hawaiian *heiau* was a rectangular court, sometimes built in terraces surrounded with a stone wall or a wood fence [96]. Inside, its most characteristic feature (apart from an offering platform and houses for priests and religious paraphernalia, as in the Society Islands) was the oracle tower, built of wood and covered with barkcloth, which was entered by priests during ceremonies to receive messages from the gods. The most important of the religious ceremonies was the annual harvest festival of *makahiki*. It was signalled by the appearance of the constellation Pleiades and lasted from October till February. The first part of the celebration was the *kapu* time, when work and war were forbidden and taxes were brought to special altars set up at district boundaries. During that time the image of Lono was taken round the islands to acknowledge the offerings. When the circuit was completed, the *kapu* was lifted and the second period started – the time of enjoyment, feasts and general merrymaking.

The festival of *makahiki* was to have particular significance in relation to Cook's arrival in Hawaii, and the resemblance of the symbol of Lono – a pole with a cross-bar from which white barkcloth sheets were suspended – to the ship's sails deepened this significance still further.

In contrast to the Society Islands, agriculture in Hawaii was a highly-skilled, systematic occupation due to the seasonal variations of the climate and difficult terrain. It was a way of life and religious ceremonies accompanied the whole agricultural cycle. The most important cultivated plant was taro, usually grown on artificial, irrigated terraces, but sweet potato, yam, breadfruit and kava were also cultivated. Fishing played a large part in the economy and required special training and skills, which were held in high regard. Fishing techniques were of the general

96 A *heiau* at Waimea, Kauai, Hawaiian Islands, by John Webber, 1778. *Add. MS 15513 f.27*

Polynesian type, with some local modifications [97]. The canoes were dug-outs with added washstrakes. They could be either double, or single with an outrigger; of the latter Captain Cook wrote: 'those that go single have out riggers, which are shaped and fited with more judgement than any I had before seen' (*ibid.*, 282–3).

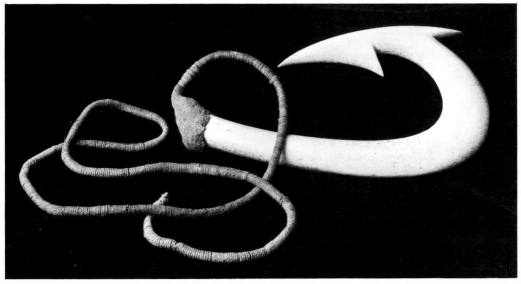

97 Bone shark-hook. Hawaiian Islands. *l.* 23 cm. *HAW 62*

98 The village of Waimea on Kauai, Hawaiian Islands, by John Webber, 1778. *Add. MS 15513 f.29*

The Hawaiians lived in villages [98], in houses which Cook described as 'not unlike oblong corn stacks' (*ibid.*, 283) with frames of wood and thatched roofs and walls. There were no windows, and 'some of our gentlemen observed that when they wanted light they made a hole in the wall and closed it again when they had done with it' (*ibid.*, 283). Cooking was done in earth ovens, as everywhere else in

Polynesia. It was men's work and the sexes ate separately. The staple food was *poi* – mashed cooked taro diluted with water – usually served with fish. Pork was eaten only on special occasions, and dog meat was reserved for the chiefs. Domestic utensils were similar to those in the Society Islands but there were no stools and instead of headrests there were plaited pillows. Wood bowls, usually very carefully

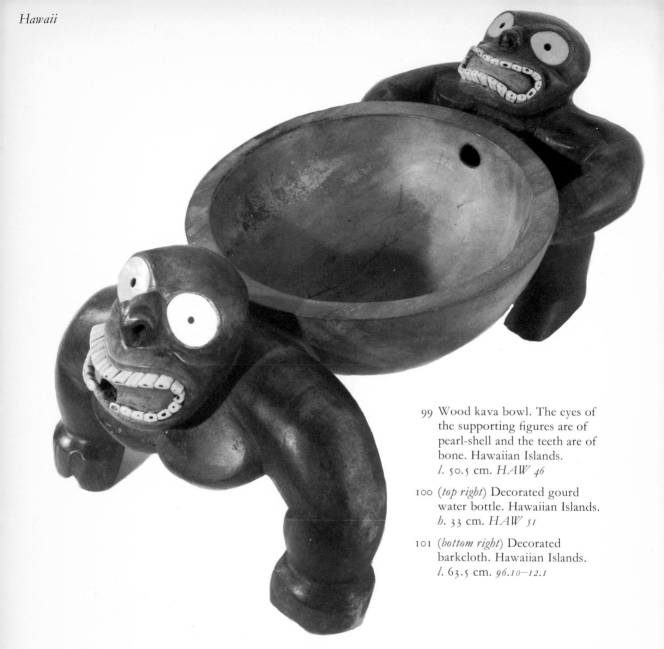

99 Wood kava bowl. The eyes of
the supporting figures are of
pearl-shell and the teeth are of
bone. Hawaiian Islands.
l. 50.5 cm. *HAW 46*

100 (*top right*) Decorated gourd
water bottle. Hawaiian Islands.
h. 33 cm. *HAW 51*

101 (*bottom right*) Decorated
barkcloth. Hawaiian Islands.
l. 63.5 cm. *96.10−12.1*

finished, were common and gourd water bottles were often decorated [**99, 100**].
Basic tools were like those in the rest of Polynesia – stone adzes and chisels, shell
scrapers, bamboo knives. Clothes were made of barkcloth (a loin cloth, *malo*, for
men, and a knee-length skirt, *pa'u*, for women, with a shawl or mantle, *kihei*, in
colder weather for both sexes) which was beautifully decorated with natural dyes
[**101**]; indeed ornamented barkcloth is one of the greatest artistic achievements of
the Hawaiian culture. Cook was unusually effusive in his praise: 'But what they most
excell in colouring is cloth . . . none of it is remarkably fine but it is all glazed and
prented with different Colours, which are so disposed as to have a pritty and pleasing

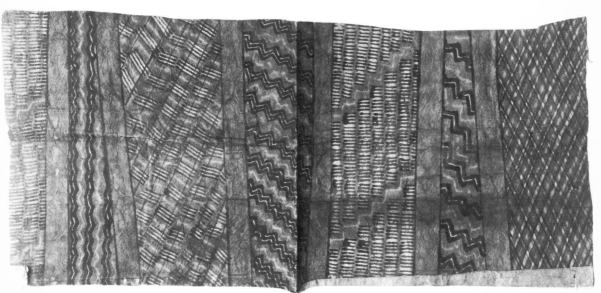

103 Feather neck ornaments. Hawaiian Islands. *l.* 40.5 cm. *HAW 114*

effect; they have a very great variety of patterns and many of them are extremely beautifull' (*ibid.*, 283). The decorating was done with the help of bamboo liners (though later a printing technique, using bamboo stamps, was developed). Personal ornaments consisted mainly of necklaces, *lei*, made of shell, seeds, whale ivory and feathers [**103**], the latter being women's most precious possessions [**102**], and of bracelets made of turtle shell or boar tusks [**104**]. Tattooing was practised but it was limited to simple, geometric patterns.

104 Bracelet of boar's tusks. Hawaiian Islands. *h.* 8.5 cm. *HAW 156*

105 Feather cloak. Hawaiian Islands. *w.* 203 cm. *NN. Not from Cook's voyages*

106 Feather cape. Hawaiian Islands. *w.* 114 cm. *NN*

Chiefs wore special garments for ceremonial occasions. These were capes, cloaks and helmets covered with feathers. The cloaks [**105**] and capes [**106**] had a netting foundation made of vegetable fibre, to which the feathers, tied in little bunches, were attached. They were called *'ahu'ula*, which means 'red garments' (red was a sacred colour throughout Polynesia), but the most valued were the ones with predominance of yellow feathers, due to their greater scarcity. The helmets, *mahiole* [Plate XIII], were made of basketry, and then covered with netting or a braid, arranged in successive layers, to which the feathers were attached. Cook wrote: 'They have also neat Tippets made of red and yellow feathers, and Caps and Cloaks covered with the same or some other feathers, . . . These [the caps] and also the cloaks they set so high a Value upon that I could not procure one, some were however got' (*ibid.*, 280). A Chief's regalia was completed by a feathered staff of state, *kahili* [**107**], with a handle of wood, bone or turtle shell.

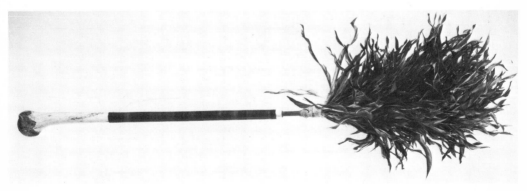

[119]

107 Feather staff of state with bone handle. Hawaiian Islands. *l.* 89 cm. *HAW 167*

The chiefs wore these ceremonial garments in battle, where they served as a rallying point for the warriors. Wars were frequent in Hawaii, as in the Society Islands, and largely for the same reasons. Warfare was similarly formalised and accompanied by religious ritual. Battles were fought in open country, in daylight, in a straightforward manner. Weapons included spears [108], daggers, clubs and shark

108 Barbed wood spear (detail), said to have been thrown into the boat when Cook was killed, and brought back to England by Thomas Bean, a member of the crew of the *Discovery*. Hawaiian Islands. *l.* 261.5 cm (whole spear). *1946 Oc.1.1*

tooth weapons. Slings and tripping weapons were also used. Professional warriors, *koa*, a small body of whom was usually kept by a chief at his court, acted as champions. Women sometimes accompanied men into battle to be on hand in case they were wounded. The chief, in the centre of his army, was accompanied by priests carrying feather images of gods [Plates XI, XII], probably representing Ku. They were fashioned out of basketry, somewhat like the helmets, and covered with netting with feathers attached. They had pearl-shell eyes and dog's teeth. These feather gods were unique to Hawaii. Featherwork in general is another great achievement of Hawaiian creativity and although feather garments were made elsewhere in Polynesia, nowhere did the craft reach a comparable degree of excellence [Plate XIV].

Wood carving was another skill in which the Hawaiians excelled but the style of their carving was quite different from that of the Maori; for the Hawaiians the form, not ornamentation, was important. For example, wooden bowls, beautifully finished with elegant, simple lines were never decorated with surface carving, though those used by chiefs sometimes had human figure supports [99]. Drums could also have such supports [109]. Hawaiian wood carving found its highest expression in images of the gods, among which the most magnificent were large temple images devoid of any surface decoration. They were characterised by exaggerated musculature of the body and discrete planes, often retaining marks of adze strokes. They convey a sense of power, aggression and controlled dynamism. Smaller, portable figures tended to be finished more carefully with a greater variety of style. This is also true of free-standing images, which are also more realistic. Some of them have pearl-shell eyes, human teeth and hair pegged in.

109 Wood drum with
sharkskin membrane
and base carved
as human figures.
Hawaiian Islands.
h. 29 cm. *1977 Oc.8.1*

110 Gourd rattle decorated with feathers. Hawaiian Islands. *d.* 45.5 cm. *HAW 93*

Like all Polynesians, the Hawaiians were fond of dancing, singing and games. Music, dance and poetry were closely linked in the *hula* ceremony, in which dancing was accompanied by chanting and drumming. *Hula* had a religious meaning and expert performers spent a long time in secluded training in preparation for the ceremony. Musical instruments consisted of wood drums, similar to those of the Society Islands, gourd and small coconut drums, gourd rattles, sometimes decorated with feathers [**110**], nose flutes, shell trumpets and musical bows. Competitive games of various sorts were very popular. The Hawaiians were also excellent sportsmen. There was boxing, wrestling, racing and, the most spectacular of all, surfing. They were also unsurpassed swimmers. Captain Cook wrote: 'the most expert swimmers we had met with . . . It was very common for women with infants at the breast to come off in Canoes to look at the Ships, and when the surf was so high that they could not land them in the Canoes they used to leap over board with the child in their arms and make their way a shore through a surf that looked dreadfull' (*ibid.*, 281).

The name Cook gave the archipelago was the Sandwich Islands, in honour of the First Lord of the Admiralty. Some of his men had doubts whether they were indeed the first ships to visit the islands because of the presence of iron (there were a few pieces of it used as tools) but Cook, rightly, came to the conclusion that these pieces had reached the islands lodged in driftwood. Besides, 'the very great surprise they shewed at the sight of the ships and their total ignorance of fire arms seemd to prove the contrary' [i.e. that it was indeed the first European visit] (*ibid.*, 285).

When the ships anchored off Kauai, Cook went ashore. 'The very instant I leaped ashore, they all fell flat on their faces, and remained in that humble posture till I made signs to them to rise' (*ibid.*, 269). Such prostration was a mark of respect and submission paid to the highest chiefs, and was to be a part of the extraordinary homage and respect which Cook was to receive continually in Hawaii.

The first visit was very short, only a fortnight, during which Cook went ashore three times. It is amazing how much he observed and recorded about the people. He liked the Hawaiians, 'an open, candid, active people' (*ibid.*, 281), he thought them honest: 'No people could trade with more honisty . . . Some indeed at first betrayed a thievish disposition, or rather they thought they had a right to any thing they could lay their hands upon but this conduct they soon laid aside' (*ibid.*, 272). This was not quite true, as became obvious when the ships returned to Hawaii. In fact in one incident the Hawaiians excelled themselves: when a pewter dish with food was sent to a watering party on shore through a Hawaiian helper, the man appropriated the dish and sold its contents to the seamen 'who swore Damn their Eyes that these black Buggers understand roasting of hogs as well as we do', as Edgar, master of the *Discovery*, put it succinctly (*ibid.*, 272, f.2).

The ships returned to Hawaii in the second half of November 1778, after visiting the Arctic Ocean, and cruised off the islands for seven weeks before anchoring. Cook's purpose – apart from looking for a good anchorage – was to control trading and to prevent transmission of disease to the local people, but this delay was a tremendous strain on his crew after their trying time in the north, and they were disgruntled. However, all this time a constant supply of fresh food was brought to the ships in canoes together with women whom 'it was not possible to keep . . . out of the Ship and no women I ever met with were more ready to bestow their favours, indeed it appeared to me that they came with no other view' (*ibid.*, 486). Eventually the ships anchored on 17 January at Kealakekua Bay in Hawaii. The same day Cook went ashore with King, accompanied by local chiefs and priests. He was conducted to a *heiau* where (according to King's journal, for Cook's journal breaks off at this point), at a long and complex ceremony he was acknowledged as an incarnation of Lono. The facts that the time of the ships' arrival coincided with the festival of *makahiki*, and that the ships' sails resembled the image of Lono have already been mentioned. To them must be added that the Hawaiians had traditions foretelling the coming of Lono, so that there is little doubt that Cook was indeed accepted as the god. The ceremony itself was not without some lighter moments; at one stage Cook and King were ceremonially fed, and King wrote: 'I had no objection to have the hog handled by Pareea, but the Captn recollecting what offices Koah had officiated when he handled the Putrid hog could not get a Morsel down, not even when the old fellow very Politely chew'd it for him' (*ibid.*, 506).

From then on whenever Cook went ashore, he was received by the priests, food offerings were brought to him, and the people prostrated themselves. King said 'It is very clear . . . that they regard us as a Set of beings infinitely their superiors' (*ibid.*, 525). The supreme chief Kalani'opu'u paid Cook a visit bringing feather gods with him, but he did not come on board. Instead, Cook followed him ashore, where the chief 'threw in a graceful manner over the Captns Shoulders the Cloak he himself wore' (*ibid.*, 512). He was also given a helmet and a feathered staff, *kahili*, while five or six cloaks were laid at his feet, 'all very beautiful, & to them of the greatest Value' (*ibid.*, 512). The ceremony ended with the presentation of some more foodstuffs to Cook. King himself must have been very much liked, for the chiefs asked Cook to leave him behind. King wrote: 'I had had proposals by our friends to elope, & they promised to hide me in the hills till the Ships were gone, & to make me a great man' (*ibid.*, 518–19). The ships left Hawaii on 4 February, and the departing Europeans took away with them a very favourable impression of the Hawaiians.

As luck would have it, four days after leaving the bay, they ran into a gale and the *Resolution*'s foremast head was badly sprung. To repair it, the mast would have to be taken out of the ship, and Cook had no choice but to return to Kealakekua Bay where work on the mast was started at once. The priests were cooperative but the chiefs were very inquisitive about the reasons for the ships' return. Although superficially things went on as before, the attitude of the Hawaiians changed. They were disrespectful and insolent, interfered with the seamens' work and threw stones at them; annoying incidents of theft increased until Cook had had enough: 'the Captn expressd his sorrow, that the behaviour of the Indians would at last oblige him to use force; for that they must not he said imagine they have gaind an advantage over us', recorded King (*ibid.*, 530). Cook's determination was put to the test the following day, 14 February. In the morning it was found that the *Discovery*'s cutter was stolen. Cook sent boats off to blockade the bay till the cutter was returned and he himself, with a party of marines, set out to take the chief Kalani'opu'u hostage. When they landed, the boats were left near the shore, and Cook with one officer and nine marines went to the village. The chief, who knew nothing of the theft, readily agreed to come with Cook, but when they were walking down the beach to the boats, he was stopped by his wife and some chiefs who implored him not to go. The old chief became confused, Cook continued to insist, and the Hawaiians, already alarmed by the Europeans' unusual manner and all the muskets, became hostile. Cook now realised that he had to abandon his plan and let the chief go, for to carry it through would mean too great a loss of Hawaiian lives. He said to Phillips, the officer who was with him: 'We can never think of compelling him to go onboard without killing a number of these People' (*ibid.*, 535). He and his party were going towards the shore to embark when the news arrived that a shot from the boats blockading the bay had killed an important chief. The Hawaiians were enraged; one man threatened Cook with a dagger, he retaliated by firing small shot which did the man no harm but only provoked him further. At this the rest of the Hawaiians joined in, stabbing and throwing stones. Cook fired a ball and killed a man, the marines fired, but were overwhelmed before they had a chance to reload. Cook gave an order to take to the boats, and, on turning his back to the crowd to wave the boats to come in or to stop firing, he was hit from behind [111]. He staggered, was stabbed and fell face down into the water. The Hawaiians surged forward and he disappeared from view engulfed by the crowd. A few marines and Phillips managed to reach the boats which pulled off leaving Cook and four marines dead on the beach.

Cook's death was most probably the result of an unfortunate coincidence of circumstances, and the Hawaiian aggression was most probably quite unpremeditated, breaking out on the spur of the moment. Cook had been in danger before, in Tonga and Raiatea, where there were plots to seize him; he had been in circumstances similar to those in Kealakekua Bay and his practice of taking hostages was an old and tried one. But on this occasion he acted more rashly than usual and he seemed to have lost his customary understanding and sensitivity to the moods and attitudes of the local people. It was his third voyage, he had already shown signs of stress in the Society Islands, and now perhaps he was exasperated beyond endurance with the eternal thieving and meant to put a stop to it once and for all. But he underestimated the Hawaiians' loyalty to their chief, their extraordinary courage when faced with firearms, and their exasperation with the European visitors who kept coming back for more and more of their limited food supplies.

The fact remains that even after his death the Hawaiians still saw Cook as a supernatural being, asking whether he would ever come again. His body was treated in the manner reserved for the highest chiefs; parts of it were burned and the head and limbs were distributed among the important chiefs and priests as relics.

Clerke, who now took over command, decided against retaliation, in spite of pressure from the seamen and some of his officers. He insisted however on Cook's body being returned, and waited while the repairs on the mast continued. But there was much bitterness between the Europeans and the Hawaiians, and King wrote: 'Our people in this days transactions did many reprehensible things; in excuse of

111 (*overleaf*) The Death of Captain Cook, engraved by F. Bartolozzi and W. Byrne after the drawing by John Webber, 1784. *1870–5–14–2136*

which it can only be said that their minds were strongly agitat'd at the barbarous manner in which the Captn was treated, & they were very desirous of taking ample Vengeance' (*ibid.*, 562). The Hawaiians, subdued and unhappy, grieved over Cook's death nearly as much as the Europeans. Slowly the old friendship was patched up, at least amongst the officers, and chiefs and priests. Cook's remains were returned and committed to the sea. On 22 February the ships sailed out of Kealakekua Bay, and on 15 March they left the archipelago behind on their way to a second spell of exploration in the north. King, in his final evaluation of the sad events, wrote: 'From all our Transactions, we must I think allow the Natural dispositions of these people to be good, & in this point they are like their Brethren at the Society & Friendly Islands. I do not see that their conduct when we were at open hostilities ought to be brought as any Proof to the Contrary . . . when their Passions had time to Cool, & they saw the folly of their Opposition, they gave us many marks of their being sorry at what had happen'd, & gave us that test of former friendship by putting themselves in our power, & as good a proof as could be given, without an actual experiment, that had we been in theirs, we should have been safe' (*ibid.*, 612–13).

6 Conclusion

HELEN WALLIS

WHEN *A Voyage to the Pacific Ocean* was published on King George III's fortieth birthday, 4 June 1784, the results of Captain Cook's three voyages could be assessed as a whole. As editor of the second and third voyages Canon John Douglas was well placed to appreciate their significance. In his long and much praised preface, he commented, 'But while our late voyages have opened so many channels to an increase of knowledge . . . let us not forget another very important object of study, for which they have afforded to the speculative philosopher ample materials: I mean the study of human nature'. He saw the Pacific islands as 'a fit soil from whence a careful observer could collect facts for forming a judgement, how far unassisted human nature will be apt to degenerate; and in what respects it can ever be able to excel' (Cook and King, 1784, I, lxvii–lxviii). Looking back from the twentieth century it may seem that this remarkable era of Pacific discovery was comparable to the discovery of America nearly two hundred years earlier. Yet there was one important difference. It took several decades for the shape of the American continent to become known, and most Europeans of the late fifteenth and early sixteenth centuries lived and died with only the vaguest notions of the 'new found lands'. Europeans of the 1770s were aware that they were spectators of a great historical event, the unveiling of a new world. Printed accounts, pictures and engravings, a wealth of natural history specimens, and a new class of specimens called 'artificial curiosities', were available to instruct and entertain, while for the natural philosopher there were new and complex manifestations of human nature for speculative study.

From Magellan in 1521 to Bougainville in 1768, as H. E. Maude points out ('Pacific History – past, present and future', *Journal of Pacific History*, 6(1971), 12–13) the information learnt about the peoples of the Pacific was limited by the absence of any adequate means of verbal communication so that only what could be observed of the material culture and the visual manifestations of social behaviour could be recorded, while beliefs and motivations remained a closed book. On Cook's voyages, with the beginning of a rudimentary verbal communication, terms were given for objects and ceremonies, and events were described through an interchange of ideas. Because the visits were short the islanders tended to be seen under conditions of excitement and stress, and observations were necessarily somewhat distorted. Nevertheless, a communication beyond the material plane was established. Thus the moment in history when Cook approached Vahitahi Atoll in the Tuamotu Archipelago in April 1769 can be seen as marking the beginning of Pacific ethnography.

The London public gained their first glimpse of life in the South Seas in the pages of the *General Evening Post* and of the *Middlesex Chronicle* of 29 July 1771, both of which carried the same report of Cook's visit to Tahiti in 1769: 'An Authentic Account of the Natives of Otahittee or George's Island . . .'. For the full official account of the First Voyage they had to await the publication (in May 1773) of 'Hawkesworth's *Voyages*,' as the work became popularly known. Despite the controversy which filled the correspondence columns of the newspapers during the next few months on the subject of Hawkesworth's editorial skills and rewards, the *Voyages* were an immediate best-seller. One correspondent who called himself 'a Seaman', summed up his impressions very fairly as follows: 'It may be called a real authentic Account of a new World, such as no European could have figured in his own Imagination'.

This 'authentic' account was in fact edited and altered according to the subjective interpretations of observer and editor, themselves influenced by current European preconceptions. For the First Voyage the greatest centre of interest was Tahiti and the Society Islands. Banks had seen Tahiti as a terrestrial paradise, 'this Land of Liberty', the island 'where Love is the Chief Occupation' (Beaglehole, 1963, ii, 330–1). Hawkesworth in his turn found Banks's elegant descriptions more to his taste than Cook's plain words. 'The whole scene realizes the poetic fables of Arcadia', Hawkesworth wrote, echoing Banks in describing the first impressions of Tahiti (Hawkesworth, 1773, ii, 83; Beaglehole, 1963, ii, 252). Comparisons with ancient Greece became a favourite theme. 'The Indians like Homer of old must be poets as well as musicians', Banks wrote of the travelling musicians, a company of *arioi* (*ibid.*, i, 290), and Hawkesworth called them 'The bards and minstrels of Otaheite'. The first European visitors to Polynesia tended to view the natives as noble savages, an attitude with its roots deep in the thought of classical antiquity (Smith, 1960, 6, 70). The neo-classical movement of the day thus influenced initial impressions. The Society Islanders were seen as 'soft primitives', living an idyllic life in a tropical paradise; the Fuegians, Maoris and Australian aborigines as hard 'primitives', who in a harsher environment were at a lower, more barbaric level of development. Lord Monboddo, moreover, elaborated these ideas into a general

INHABITANTS *of the Island of* **TERRA·DEL FUEGO** *in their Hut.*

112 Tierra del Fuegans in their hut, by Alexander Buchan, 1769, with, below, the engraved version by Bartolozzi after Cipriani. *Add. MS 23920 f.14*

113 A boat-house on Raiatea ('Ulietea'), Society Islands, after a drawing by Sydney Parkinson, 1769

theory of evolution, drawing extensively on the South Sea discoveries as evidence, alleging 'the golden age may be said yet to exist in some of the countries that have been discovered in the South Sea, where the inhabitants live, without toil or labour, upon the bounty of nature in these fine climates'.

The illustrations in Hawkesworth's *Voyages* exploited and encouraged these preconceptions. Banks's artists Alexander Buchan and Sydney Parkinson were men noted for their accuracy of delineation. Buchan was to draw 'savages' and scenery, Parkinson the plants and animals, but Buchan's illness and subsequent death at Tahiti left Parkinson reponsible for both types of work, and Parkinson himself did

Note the classicised attitudes of the figures. *Hawkesworth, 1773, plate 3*

not survive the voyage. At the hands of the artists and engravers entrusted with the preparation of the plates, subtle and blatant distortions of scene and mood were effected. The alterations made by Giovanni Batista Cipriani to Buchan's sketch of the Fuegians and by Rooker to Parkinson's sketch of a canoe and a canoe shed on Ulietea (Raiatea) are the most notorious examples (Hawkesworth, 1773, II, no. 3) [112, 113]. The Maori chief (*ibid.*, III, no. 13) [114], on the other hand, was rendered more or less without alteration and is notable as the only engraving in Hawkesworth in which native figures are not subject to some kind of idealising by engravers (Smith, 1960, 24).

[133]

The Admiralty learnt its lesson from the controversy over Hawkesworth's *Voyages*. For the second voyage the public were allowed to read Cook's own words. Of all three voyages this is the text most faithful to Cook's journals: 'It is my own narrative, and as it was written during the voyage' (Beaglehole, 1961, cxliii). Canon Douglas's editing was anonymous and discreet, and both men were mindful of the susceptibilities of 'the nicest readers', whom Hawkesworth had offended with his forthright accounts of Tahitian social customs. The two volumes published in May 1777 met with immediate success. For this voyage the artist was William Hodges, a pupil of Richard Wilson, a landscape painter of distinction. He was an experimental artist, and was especially concerned with the expression of natural phenomena such as meteorological effects. His drawings also were subjected to distortion by the artists preparing the work for the engraver. Once again Cipriani's hand can be detected as author of the most absurd of the transformations: that suffered by the Landing at Middleburgh. George Forster, mistakenly, took Hodges to task: 'The plates which ornamented the history of captain Cook's former voyage, have been justly criticised, because they exhibited to our eyes the pleasing forms of antique figures and draperies, instead of Indians of which we wished to form some idea. But it is also greatly to be feared, that Mr. Hodges has lost the sketches and drawings which he made from NATURE in the course of the voyage, and supplied the deficiency in this case, from his own elegant ideas. The connoisseur will find Greek contours and features in this picture, which had never existed in the South Sea'. (George Forster, *A Voyage round the World*, London, 1777, vol. 1, 427–8; **115**).

The neo-classical interpretations were now being challenged as knowledge of the Pacific islanders increased. George Forster's own two-volume account of the Voyage, produced in 1777 as a rival publication to Cook's, is notable for its determined attitude of scientific detachment. A year later this was complemented by Johann Reinhold Forster's *Observations made during a Voyage round the World, on Physical Geography, Natural History, and Ethic Philosophy*, London, 1778: a massive volume which can be regarded as the first ethnographical treatise on the South Seas.

For the third voyage, tragically, there was no Captain Cook to look over Canon Douglas's shoulder. 'The Cap!'s M.S.S. was indeed attended to accurately; but I took more liberties than I had done with his Acc! of the second Voyage', Douglas wrote. The work on the plates explains why publication was delayed until 1784. The edition was sold out in three days and a second immediately commissioned by the Admiralty. It can be claimed that no other voyage of any nation had been recorded with such care and expense. From Lord Hardwicke, teased for his 'spite against the South Sea' (as Daniel Wray called it), the illustrations won high praise: 'I do not wonder that the Plates are first looked over', he wrote to Douglas, 'as they are the best performed of any annexed to the Discoverys of that unfortunate Officer'.

114 Portrait of a New Zealand Maori man, by
Sydney Parkinson, 1770, with, below, the
engraved version. *Add. MS 23920 f.54*

115 The landing at Middleburgh [Eua, Tonga]. Engraved by J. K. Shirwin, 1777, after a painting by William Hodges.

The outstanding quality of the engravings arose from several factors. John Webber, artist for the third voyage, was a prolific worker and no voyage undertaken in the days before photography ever returned so well documented with pictorial illustrations (Smith, 1960, 78). Nor had so great an area of the earth's surface ever before come under one artist's observation. There was the further advantage that Webber himself supervised the work on the engravings, comprising sixty-one engraved plates after his original drawings. The engravings achieved immediate fame. Johann Gottfried von Herder wrote: 'Cook's last voyage, if we may trust what

Fame says of its engravings, commences a new and higher period, the continuation of which in other parts of the world I ardently desire' (*Outlines of a Philosophy of the History of Man*, 1800, 289). The plates, together with those for the first two voyages, were much copied and became standard illustrations for the Pacific (British Museum, 1979, 9 ff.).

The vivid accounts and depictions of sights and scenes of the Pacific available to the public in these publications were supplemented by the material objects brought home, natural and artificial. They included many hundreds of herbarium specimens

together with drawings and manuscripts, which represented new genera and species, as W. T. Stearn has shown. The resulting publications were disappointing. For one reason or another Banks never had his *Florilegium* published, although 742 copper plates were engraved from Parkinson's drawings, and can be described as 'masterpieces of the engraver's art'. The botanical records of the second voyage prepared by the Forsters, and produced in a folio volume entitled *Characteres Generum Plantarum . . . (1775)* were printed in only six copies.

The collections of objects were eagerly sought after by museums and private collectors. Sir Ashton Lever's museum – the Leverian Museum – which in 1781 received a large collection from Captain Cook's third voyage, was one of the most famous of the private museums. Another, William Bullock's museum, moved from Liverpool to London in 1809, and added to its collections by purchasing from the 1806 auction of the Leverian Museum collection. In the British Museum the Otaheite and South Sea Rooms were among the popular sights of London, as J. P. Malcolm reports in his *Londinium Redivivum*, vol. 2 (1803), 520–8. It is interesting to note that Douglas in his Introduction now sought to entice the reader away from the perusal of Greek and Roman antiquities, 'But will not his curiosity be more awakened . . . by passing an hour in surveying the numerous specimens of the ingenuity of our newly-discovered friends, brought from the utmost recesses of the globe, to enrich the British Museum and the valuable repository of Sir Ashton Lever? . . . the *novelties* of the Society or Sandwich Islands, seem better calculated to engage the attention of the studious of our times, than the *antiquities*, which exhibited proofs of Roman magnificence' (Cook and King, 1784, 1, lxix).

London Society was also diverted by the presence in their midst of a living specimen, so to speak, in the person of Omai, 'Pacific envoy' [50, 116], as he has been called by his recent biographer, E. H. McCormick. Philosophical comments on the life of the South Seas islanders were given a focal point in Omai, famous for his alleged 'How do, King Tosh'. Many satirical words on European Society were printed as if from his pen, in condemnation of the luxuries of Europe as opposed to the simple life of the South Seas. The following lines in *An Historic Epistle, from Omiah to the Queen of Otaheite; being his Remarks on the English Nation* (1775), illustrate the treatment:

> *Can* Europe *boast, with all her pilfer'd wealth*
> *A larger store of happiness, or health?*
> *What then avail her thousand arts to gain*
> *The store of every land and every main;*
> *Whilst we, whom love's more grateful joys enthrall,*
> *Profess one art – to live without them all.*

[139]

16 Omai, engraved by L. Jacobi, 1777, after the portrait by
Sir Joshua Reynolds in the Castle Howard collection.

The poet contrasts the simple life of the South Seas with the complexity of English society:

> *Not rul'd like us on nature's simple plan,*
> *Here laws on laws perplex the dubious man.*

Omai was also the vehicle for John O'Keeffe's play, *Omai: or a Trip round the World*, the Christmas pantomime at the Theatre Royal, Covent Garden in 1785 (British Museum, 1979, 81 ff.). A great success, it ran to fifty performances in one season, including a Royal Command performance. Costume and decor were in the hands of Philippe de Loutherbourg, whose scenes were based on engravings after Webber and Hodges. The exotic landscapes and peoples set a new theme for theatrical productions. Its scenario encompassed the world, ranging from the 'bay of Otaheite', to London, Kamchatka, Tongatabu and Hawaii. The final scenes featured a magnificent procession of the nations, and ended with an *apotheosis* of Captain Cook, crowned by Fame and Britannia [**117**]. Not to be outdone, Paris followed in October 1788 with *La Mort du Captaine Cook*, a 'serious-pantomimic-ballet' by M. Arnould, which came to the Theatre Royal, Covent Garden in 1789. Set entirely in Hawaii, this concluded with a solemn funeral ceremony in which the Hawaiians mourn Captain Cook's death.

The theme of Captain Cook as a tragic hero heightened the effect of the drama of the encounter between Europe and the South Seas. Cook and the idealised 'savage' confronted each other in a moment of classical tragedy, and in this encounter the Noble Savage becomes 'the inglorious native' (Smith, 1960, 86). But another interpretation of the encounter appeared very early in the proceedings, the theme of 'the injured islanders'. George Forster was one of the first to see the coming of Europeans as a source of corruption to Polynesian society. 'It were indeed sincerely to be wished, that the intercourse which has lately subsisted between Europeans and the natives of the South Sea islands may be broken off in time, before the corruption of manners which unhappily characterises civilised regions, may reach that innocent race of men, who live here fortunate in their ignorance and simplicity. But it is a melancholy truth that the dictates of philanthropy do not harmonise with the political systems of Europe' (Forster, 1777, I, 303). He anticipates that inequalities of class may develop in Tahitian society in place of what he saw (mistakenly) as 'a happy equality': 'If the knowledge of a few individuals can only be acquired at such a price as the happiness of nations, it were better for the discoverers and the discovered, that the South Sea had still remained unknown to Europe and its restless inhabitants' (*ibid.*, I, 368).

It may have been Forster's influence which led Cook to speculate, 'Tell me what the Natives of the whole extent of America have gained by the commerce they have

117 The Apotheosis of Captain Cook b[y]
Philippe de Loutherbourg, 1794.

The APOTHEOSIS of CAPTAIN COOK.

From a Design of P.J.De Loutherbourg, R.A. The View of KARAKAKOOA BAY
Is from a Drawing by John Webber, R.A the last he made in the Collection of M.ʳ G.Baker.

London, Pub.ᵈ Jan.ʳ 20. 1794, by J.Thane, Spur Strat, Leicester Square.

had with Europeans' (Beaglehole, 1961, 167). Forster's ideas in turn inspired Gerald Fitzgerald's poem *The Injured Islanders, or the influence of art upon the happiness of Nature* (1779). This time the poetical epistle was from Oberea of Otaheite and was addressed to Captain Wallis:

> *Yes,* WALLIS*! yes, this last – this worst of woes*
> *From boasted Europe's baneful commerce flows,*
> *Some vagrant chief, of ever hateful name,*
> *Approach'd our isle, and spread the wasting flame.*

This is a reference to the introduction of venereal disease, which Hawkesworth attributed to Bougainville's visit, but which might first have been introduced by Wallis's men.

Here was the paradox. As the science of ethnography had its birth, Europeans began to perceive the solemn truth, that they were participants as well as observers. 'Ethnology is in a sadly ludicrous, not to say tragic, position, that at the very moment when it begins to put its workshop in order . . . the material of its study melts away with hopeless rapidity . . . when men fully trained for the work have begun to travel into savage countries and study their inhabitants – these die away under our very eyes'. Thus Bronislaw Malinowski wrote in his foreword to *Argonauts of the Western Pacific*, 1932. The introduction of European disease and of the use of fire-arms were two of the more sinister results of the European invasion of the Pacific, while the well-intentioned work of the missionaries removed the lynch-pin of social activity, religion and its attendant ritual, leaving no comparable focus in its place.

In every area the story was the same: native populations diminished (in Tahiti, for example, the estimated 40,000 inhabitants in Cook's time dwindled at one point to a mere 6000); thus the Old World, in the form of a succession of explorers, traders, evangelists and settlers, hastening eagerly in Cook's tracks, in the end all but destroyed the New World he had revealed to enchant and edify the *cognoscenti* of Europe in that remarkable decade, 1770–1780. In the present times we begin to realise the nature of what has been lost or destroyed and, from an informed evaluation of the first-hand accounts of the Pacific world as it was then found, we gain an historical perspective on its 'natural and artificial curiosities'; they were relics of doomed cultures. It seems a curious irony that when Banks and Solander dried their botanical specimens on the first voyage, they placed them in proof sheets of Joseph Addison's commentary on Milton's *Paradise Lost*.

References and Abbreviations

All the objects illustrated were collected on one of the three voyages of Captain Cook unless it is stated to the contrary. Bracketed figures in the text refer to illustrations. All the photographs, except those credited otherwise, were taken by the photographic services of the British Library Reference Division (drawings etc.) or of the British Museum (objects).

l. = length; *h.* = height; *w.* = width; *d.* = diameter

Beaglehole, 1955, 1961, 1967, 1974: Beaglehole, J. C., ed., *The Journals of Captain James Cook on his Voyages of Discovery*. Cambridge and London for the Hakluyt Society, 1955–1974. Vol.1 The Voyage of the *Endeavour* 1768–1771, 1955; Vol.2 The Voyage of the *Resolution* and *Adventure* 1772–1775, 1961; Vol.3 The Voyage of the *Resolution* and *Discovery* 1776–1780, 2 parts 1967; Vol.4 The Life of Captain James Cook, 1974.

Beaglehole, 1963. Beaglehole, J. C., ed., *The Endeavour Journal of Joseph Banks*. 2 vols, Sydney, 2nd ed. 1963.

British Museum, 1979: Mitchell, T. C., ed. *Captain Cook and the South Pacific* (British Museum, Yearbook 3). London, 1979.

Cook and King, 1784: Douglas, John, ed., *A Voyage to the Pacific Ocean in the years 1776, 1777, 1778, 1779 and 1780 . . . Vol. I and II written by Captain J. Cook, Vol.III by Captain J. King.* 3 vols, London, 1784.

Forster, 1778: Forster, J. R. *Observations made during a Voyage . . .* London, 1778.

Hawkesworth, 1773: Hawkesworth, John, *An Account of the Voyages undertaken for making Discoveries in the Southern Hemisphere.* 3 vols, London, 1773.

Marra, 1775: Marra, John, *Journal of the Resolution's Voyage in 1772, 1773, 1774, and 1775.* London, 1775.

Parkinson, 1773: Parkinson, Stansfield, ed., *A Journal of a voyage to the South Seas, in His Majesty's Ship, the Endeavour.* London, 1773.

Smith, 1960: Smith, Bernard, *European Vision and The South Pacific.* Oxford, 1960.